About the Author

Willis Turner has served as the President & CEO of SMEI, the worldwide professional association for sales and marketing for over 20 years. Willis is also an entrepreneur, author, and founder of Old Clayburn Event Services Inc. and Virtual Memorial Gatherings

Willis has embraced AI and the power of ChatGPT to help him initiate creative content ideas, improve customer service and streamline business processes.

Twitter: @willisturner
LinkedIn: www.linkedin.com/in/willisturner

Websites:
www.oldclayburn.com
www.virtualmemorialgatherings.com
www.smei.org

Copyright © 2023 by Willis Turner

All rights reserved. No part of this book may be reproduced, stored in a retrieval system, or transmitted in any form or by any means, electronic, mechanical, photocopying, recording, or otherwise, without the prior written permission of the publisher.

This textbook is protected under the copyright laws of the United States of America and other countries. Any reproduction or distribution of this textbook without the express permission of the publisher is strictly prohibited.

ISBN: 9798374238594

Imprint: Independently published

The author acknowledges the assistance of ChatGPT in writing this book, as well as the copyrighted or trademarked status and trademark owners of the following wordmarks mentioned in this work: ChatGPT.

This textbook is not affiliated with or endorsed by OpenAI or any other organization or individual mentioned within the textbook.

The Power of ChatGPT:
How to Put ChatGPT to Work for You

By Willis Turner CAE CME CSE

Old Clayburn
www.oldclayburn.com

Table of Contents

About the Author...i

What is ChatGPT 9

How ChatGPT Works 11

Leading ChatGPT Authorities 12

How to Access ChatGPT and Get Started............13

    There are several ways to access ChatGPT, including: 14

Available Interfaces Built on the ChatGPT Platform 21

Does ChatGPT have competitors? 23

The Art of the Prompt...29

    What are Prompts?..29

    How do I Use Prompts in ChatGPT?......................29

    Technique for Prompt Writing 30

    Best Practices for Utilizing Prompts in ChatGPT.....32

Top 20 Ways That ChatGPT is Being Used 34

    1)   Generating human-like text for chatbots and virtual assistants...34

    2. Answering Questions and Providing Information 38

3. Generating content such as articles, stories, and product descriptions 40

4. Summarizing and analyzing text 45

5. Translating text from one language to another . 48

6. Generating code and programming assistance .. 50

7. Personalizing and customizing content.............. 54

8. Generating creative writing prompts and exercises 58

9. Generating audio and video scripts 61

10. Generating legal and financial documents 67

11. Poetry, Lyrics and Song Title Generation 75

12. Generating jokes and humor 77

13. Generating product review and feedback 79

14. Generating customer service and support responses 82

15. Generating research papers and academic papers 84

16. Generating business plans and marketing strategies 87

17. Generating news articles and reports 90

18. Generating resumes and cover letters 93

19. Generating product or service descriptions 96

20. Generating creative and compelling ad copy ... 99

How Can Companies Improve Customer Service with ChatGPT? 103

Large Companies Using ChatGPT to Improve Customer Service 105

How Small Business can use ChatGPT to Enhance Customer Service 106

How Can Marketing Departments Use ChatGPT? 107

Companies that are Using ChatGPT in their Marketing Efforts 108

What Do Marketing Leaders Say about ChatGPT? 109

Marketing Agencies and ChatGPT 110

ChatGPT in Education 113

Examples of ChatGPT in Higher Education 114

ChatGPT in Manufacturing 118

Companies Using ChatGPT in Manufacturing 119

ChatGPT and Professional Speakers 123

ChatGPT and Business Coaches 126

Chat GPT and Sales Managers 131

ChatGPT and the Legal Profession 135

Law Firms Using ChatGPT 136

ChatGPT and Healthcare 140

Hospitals Using ChatGPT 142

ChatGPT and the Financial Industry **145**

Companies in the Financial Sector Using ChatGPT 146

The Transportation Industry and ChatGPT **149**

Examples of Transportation Companies Using ChatGPT..150

ChatGPT and Government **154**

Examples of ChatGPT use by Government Agencies 155

ChatGPT and Non-Profit Organizations............ **160**

Examples of Non-Profit Organizations Using ChatGPT..161

ChatGPT and Professional Associations **163**

Telecommunications and ChatGPT................... **167**

Telecommunications Companies Using ChatGPT .168

ChatGPT and the Entertainment Industry **172**

Examples of Companies in the Entertainment Industry Using ChatGPT 173

ChatGPT and Retail Companies........................ **177**

Examples of Retailers Using ChatGPT 178

ChatGPT and the Hospitality Industry **182**

Companies in Hospitality using ChatGPT 184

Content Creators and ChatGPT **188**

    How Top Content Creators Are Utilizing ChatGPT 190

Software Engineers and ChatGPT *195*

    Examples of Software Engineers Who Use ChatGPT 197

    ChatGPT and Writing Code...................................199

ChatGPT Limitations *203*

Top AI Experts Weigh in on ChatGPT's Limitations *206*

How I use ChatGPT *207*

    Improve Website SEO 207

    Writing Social Media Posts....................................211

    Answering Email 213

Top 20 Twitter Accounts Discussing ChatGPT *1*

What is the Future of ChatGPT? *4*

Resources: *7*

INDEX *8*

What is ChatGPT

ChatGPT (Conversational Generative Pre-trained Transformer), is a revolutionary artificial intelligence technology that is changing how businesses communicate with customers and employees. It has been called the future of customer service and communication, as it enables businesses to create bots that can respond to user queries quickly, accurately, and professionally. ChatGPT utilizes natural language processing (NLP) and machine learning (ML) technologies to enable bots to understand and respond to human requests in real time. By leveraging these technologies, ChatGPT's bots provide an automated response experience for users, enabling them to get the answers they need in seconds instead of minutes or hours.

These bots are trained to detect customer sentiment during conversations, allowing them to determine if customers have a positive or negative opinion about a specific product or service. At its core, ChatGPT makes use of deep learning algorithms to process words and sentences in order to understand the intent behind a query. This allows ChatGPT-enabled bots to accurately recognize requests and respond accordingly. This system can also be used to identify topics related to each conversation, helping companies craft messages tailored specifically for their target demographics.

ChatGPT makes use of emotion recognition technology which helps it better understand the emotions associated with a particular topic or conversation so that it can provide more effective responses. ChatGPT's powerful integration capabilities allow it to sync easily with existing business systems such as CRM software or accounting solutions; this makes it easier for businesses of all sizes leverage this technology without needing extensive technical support teams on hand at all times.

ChatGPT is making an impact by providing an intuitive and intelligent way for businesses large and small alike to connect with their customers, streamline business processes and spark creativity.

How ChatGPT Works

The way that ChatGPT works is by analyzing user input and breaking it down into its component parts. First, NLP algorithms are used to identify keywords and their relationships within the text. From here, machine learning models are employed to identify intent behind the statement, giving context to what the user is actually trying to say.

Deep learning algorithms then process this information in order to generate an appropriate response. This entire process takes place in a fraction of a second — allowing users to get their questions answered quickly and accurately without having to wait on hold for an agent or dig through long FAQs. In addition, these agents can be tailored directly to the needs of each particular organization, ensuring that they are providing effective service that matched their standards.

Thanks to its combination of speed and accuracy, ChatGPT technology has become incredibly popular among organizations looking for efficient solutions when it comes customer service or internal operations. With its ever-growing capabilities, it's clear that this technology will continue changing the face of how companies do business for years to come.

Leading ChatGPT Authorities

Some of the top authorities on ChatGPT include the team of researchers and engineers at OpenAI who developed and continue to improve the model. Some notable members of the team include:

- Ilya Sutskever, Research Scientist at OpenAI, who has made significant contributions to the field of deep learning.
- Dario Amodei, Research Scientist at OpenAI, who is one of the leading experts on AI safety and responsible AI.
- Jan Leike, Research Scientist at OpenAI, who leads the team responsible for improving GPT-3's ability to generate code and other structured data.
- Jack Clark, Policy Director at OpenAI, who is an expert in the field of AI policy and governance and has written extensively on the implications of GPT-3 and other advanced AI models.

There are many experts in the field of NLP and machine learning who have studied, used and written about GPT-3 and its variants like ChatGPT. Some of these experts include researchers and professors at universities, data scientists and engineers at companies.

How to Access ChatGPT and Get Started

Accessing and using ChatGPT technology is becoming increasingly easier for businesses of all sizes. In this chapter, we will discuss how to set up and use ChatGPT technology to optimize customer service, provide personalized product recommendations, improve online shopping experiences and gain valuable insights into customer behavior.

Before getting started, it's important to understand that there are two different types of Artificial Intelligence (AI) based ChatGPT Technology:

- Natural Language Processing (NLP). NLP is a type of AI technology that enables computers to understand human language. It involves breaking down sentences into their individual components such as words, phrases and clauses in order to analyze meaning and identify patterns.
- Deep learning algorithms are used to recognize patterns within large datasets — enabling the computer to make decisions without relying on instructions from humans.

Once you have a better understanding of these technologies, it's time to get started with setting up your own ChatGPT platform.

There are several ways to access ChatGPT, including:

1) Go to https://openai.com/ and click on the ChatGPT research release link

2) API: Developers can use the OpenAI API to access ChatGPT and integrate it into their own applications by following these steps:

   a) Sign up for an API key at https://beta.openai.com/account/api-keys
   b) Use the API key to make API calls to the OpenAI API, specifying the model and parameters for the API call.
   c) Use the API response to integrate the generated text into the developer's application.
   d) For more detailed information on how to use the API, refer to the OpenAI API documentation at https://beta.openai.com/docs/api-reference/introduction

3) OpenAI GPT-3 Playground: OpenAI provides a web-based playground for experimenting with GPT-3, which includes

the ability to interact with ChatGPT. You can access the OpenAI GPT-3 Playground by following these steps:
  a) Go to https://beta.openai.com/playground
  b) Sign in to your OpenAI account. If you don't have an account, you can sign up for one at https://beta.openai.com/signup
  c) Once you're signed in, you'll be able to access the playground and start experimenting with GPT-3.
  d) The playground allows you to input text and see how GPT-3 responds, you can also select the model's prompt and temperature settings to get different responses. You can also select the GPT-3 models available with different capabilities and language capabilities.

4) Third-Party Applications: There are a number of third-party applications and services that have integrated ChatGPT, such as chatbots and virtual assistants. Here are some examples of common third-party applications that use ChatGPT:
  a) Virtual Assistants: Many companies use ChatGPT to power virtual assistants that can answer customer questions and assist with customer service.

b) Chatbots: ChatGPT is often used to create chatbots for customer service, e-commerce and other industries.
c) Language Translation: ChatGPT can be used to translate text from one language to another.
d) Text Summarization: ChatGPT can be used to summarize long text into shorter, more manageable chunks.
e) Text completion: ChatGPT can be used to complete partially written text, such as a sentence or a paragraph.
f) Text generation: ChatGPT can be used to generate text, such as poetry, stories, song lyrics, or even news articles.
g) Sentiment Analysis: ChatGPT can be used to analyze text and determine the sentiment expressed in it (positive, negative, neutral).
h) Text classification: ChatGPT can be used to classify text into different categories, such as spam or not spam, or news or not news.
i) Virtual Interviews: ChatGPT can be used to create virtual interview experiences for job applicants.
j) Educational tools: ChatGPT can be used to create tools for language learning, such as chat-based language tutors.

It should be noted that ChatGPT is not only the most common GPT-3 based model, but also other models such as DialoGPT, DALL-E, etc. can be integrated with similar third-party applications.

5) There are many open-source libraries available that can be used to access and work with ChatGPT and other language models. Some of the most popular ones include:

   a) Hugging Face's transformers library: This library provides a large collection of pre-trained models, including GPT-3, as well as tools for fine-tuning and using the models in a variety of natural language processing tasks.
   b) TensorFlow: This library provides a wide range of tools for machine learning and deep learning, including support for natural language processing tasks.
   c) PyTorch: This library is also widely used for machine learning and deep learning, and has strong support for natural language processing tasks.
   d) NLTK: The Natural Language Toolkit (NLTK) is a library in Python that provides tools for natural language processing, including tokenization, stemming, and tagging.
   e) spaCy: This library provides a fast and efficient way to tokenize, parse, and tag text, as well as tools for named entity

recognition, part-of-speech tagging, and other natural language processing tasks.
f) Gensim: This library is a popular tool for topic modeling and document similarity analysis, and can be used to work with large amounts of text data.
g) OpenCV: OpenCV (Open Source Computer Vision) is a popular open-source library for computer vision and image processing tasks, which is widely used in the field of Artificial intelligence and machine learning.

These are just a few examples, many other libraries available that can be used for different natural language processing tasks, it depends on the specific use case and the personal preference of the developer.

6) Directly using the OpenAI's language models: OpenAI has several pre-trained language models that are available for use, some of the most notable ones include:

a) GPT-3 (Generative Pre-trained Transformer 3): This is one of the largest and most powerful language models available, with 175 billion parameters. It can be used for a wide range of natural language processing tasks, including language translation, text

summarization, and question answering.
b) GPT-2 (Generative Pre-trained Transformer 2): This model has 1.5 billion parameters and is trained on a diverse range of internet text. It can be fine-tuned for specific tasks such as text generation, text classification and language translation.
c) GPT (Generative Pre-trained Transformer): The original GPT model has significantly fewer parameters than GPT-2 and GPT-3 but still can be fine-tuned for specific tasks such as text generation, text classification and language translation.
d) DialoGPT (Generative Pre-trained Transformer for conversational response generation): This model is fine-tuned for conversational response generation and can be used to build chatbots and virtual assistants.
e) DALL-E (Generative Pre-trained Transformer for image and video generation): DALL-E is a model that is fine-tuned for image and video generation, it can be used for tasks such as image captioning, video summarization, and video captioning.
f) AdaNet: A family of models trained to perform a wide range of natural language understanding tasks,

including text classification, text generation, text summarization, and question answering.

These are some of the most notable models developed by OpenAI, but the company is continuously releasing new models, so the list is not exhaustive.

Available Interfaces Built on the ChatGPT Platform

ChatGPT offers a variety of powerful and intuitive interfaces for quickly creating sophisticated conversational AI bots. Here are a few examples:

1. Command-line interface (CLI): ChatGPT can be accessed via a command-line interface, which allows developers to quickly test and experiment with the model.
2. Application Programming Interface (API): ChatGPT can be accessed via an API, which allows developers to easily integrate the model into their own applications.
3. Web-based interface: Some companies offer web-based interfaces for ChatGPT, which allow developers to access the model through a web browser.
4. SDKs: Some companies provide SDKs for ChatGPT, which allow developers to easily access the model from within their own programming languages and frameworks.
5. Playground: Some companies provide Playground, which is an interactive interface that allows developers to test and experiment with the model by

      inputting text and receiving output from the model.
7. Notebook interface: Some companies provide Jupyter Notebook interface, which allows developers to test and experiment with the model in a notebook format, which is particularly useful for data science and machine learning tasks.
8. GUI: Some companies provide a Graphical User Interface (GUI) to interact with the model in a more user-friendly way.

In addition to these tools, ChatGPT also offers integrations with popular databases like MongoDB and Microsoft Azure SQL Database, as well as third-party applications such as Salesforce and Trello.

With these components, developers can rapidly develop custom chatbot applications to suit their specific needs. Examples of these applications range from customer service solutions or eCommerce stores to complex customer engagement systems.

Does ChatGPT have competitors?

In the world of natural language processing (NLP), ChatGPT is one of the most popular and advanced platforms. However, it has several competitors that are considered to be viable alternatives. The most notable of these are Dialogflow, Amazon Lex, Microsoft Bot Framework, and Rasa.

Here are the top 10 websites that could be considered competitors of ChatGPT

1. Wit.ai - https://wit.ai/ Wit.ai is an open source conversational AI platform developed by Facebook for building effective natural language processing-based chatbots and virtual assistants. It can be used to create bots for a variety of tasks from customer service to search assistance and voice control, with the ability to understand different languages.
2. Botkit – https://botkit.ai/ Botkit is an open source bot framework that provides developers with the tools they need to create custom chatbots and virtual assistants that integrate into messaging apps like Facebook Messenger, IBM Watson Conversation, Slack, and more.

3. Dialogflow (formerly Api.ai) - https://dialogflow.com/ Dialogflow (formerly Api.ai) is a powerful conversational AI platform developed by Google which provides developers with the tools they need to build their own custom chatbot or virtual assistant applications in minutes using natural language processing technology and machine learning algorithms.
4. Recast.AI – https://recast.ai/ Recast.AI is a Conversational AI platform designed for developers to easily create intelligent conversations without needing any programming skills or complex knowledge about artificial intelligence technologies such as natural language understanding or machine learning algorithms. It provides easy-to-use tools for building sophisticated dialog flows quickly and integrating with popular messaging services such as Twitter, Slack, Facebook Messenger and Skype among others.
5. Snatchbot - https://www.snatchbot.me/ Snatchbot is an AI-driven conversational bot platform developed by Snatchbot LLC which enables developers to build sophisticated dialog flows quickly within minutes without coding or any technical knowledge required by users.

It supports integration with popular messaging apps like Telegram, Viber, Kik, Line, Hangouts Chat, Microsoft Teams, Amazon Alexa, WeChat etc.,

6. RASA NLU - https://rasa.com/products/rasa-nlu : Rasa NLU (Natural Language Understanding) is an open source library for natural language processing which enables developers to quickly build sophisticated dialogs that are powered by machine learning algorithms trained on user data sets provided during development stage.
7. Amazon Lex – https://aws.amazon/ : Amazon Lex is an AWS service for building conversational interfaces into applications using voice and text chatbots. It provides developers with natural language processing (NLP) capabilities to help understand user requests, as well as advanced automatic speech recognition (ASR) technology to convert spoken input into text. Developers can use pre-built models and templates, or customize them to match their specific needs. Amazon Lex's deep learning pooling technology ensures that each customer experience is natural and contextually relevant. Additionally, it integrates with a variety of popular languages including Node.js,

Java, Python and C# so developers can quickly deploy their apps without having to build out an entirely new infrastructure.
8. Google Cloud Natural Language – https://cloud.google.com/natural-language/: Google Cloud Natural Language is a powerful and easy-to-use natural language processing (NLP) platform provided by Google. It enables developers to build sophisticated conversational AI applications quickly that understand user queries and respond accurately. The platform provides developers with pre-trained models on various topics like sentiment analysis, entity extraction, and intent recognition so they don't have to start from scratch. Additionally, it can be integrated with a wide variety of popular languages such as Python, Node.js, Java, and C# to make development faster and easier.
9. LUIS (Language Understanding Intelligent Service) – https://www.luis.ai/: Microsoft's LUIS (Language Understanding Intelligent Service) is a cloud-based NLP platform that enables developers to quickly build applications that understand natural language input. It provides users with a suite of pre-trained models, templates

and tools to quickly create custom conversational AI solutions that can understand user intent and accurately respond. Additionally, it integrates with popular programming languages such as Python, Node.js and JS so developers don't have to start from scratch. LUIS also offers advanced machine learning capabilities to help enhance its NLP capabilities even further. It is designed to be easy-to-use and highly scalable so businesses of any size can benefit from its powerful features.
10. Microsoft Bot Framework - https://dev.botframework.com/: Microsoft Bot Framework is an open-source software development kit that enables developers to quickly create sophisticated conversational AI chatbots. It provides a comprehensive platform with a wide range of features, including natural language processing (NLP), automatic speech recognition (ASR), and machine learning algorithms. Developers can take advantage of its easy-to-use tools, templates and APIs to rapidly develop chatbot applications for any use case. Additionally, it integrates with popular databases like Azure SQL Database, MongoDB and Apache CouchDB for storing conversation data. The Microsoft

Bot Framework is an effective tool for quickly building interactive, contextually intelligent bots that make the customer experience more enjoyable.

The Art of the Prompt

Prompts are an effective way of providing guidance and direction to conversational AI applications, enabling users to quickly receive responses from the system without needing to provide complex inputs. In this chapter, we will explore how to leverage prompts in ChatGPT for natural language processing (NLP) tasks, such as understanding user input and generating conversation-based responses.

The key to successfully using ChatGPT will be learning the art of the prompt.

What are Prompts?

Prompts are snippets of pre-written text that can be used as a starting point for conversations between a user and an AI application. Prompts are most often used to guide the user through a conversation by helping them formulate their thoughts or ask specific questions. Prompts can also be utilized as hints or suggestions for what type of input the AI system is expecting in order to process the given information accurately.

How do I Use Prompts in ChatGPT?

Prompts can be incorporated into ChatGPT by adding them as part of your bot's response template. For example, if you have a chatbot that responds with "What can I help you with today?" when it detects an incoming message from a user, you could also include several other variations of this prompt within the template, such as: "How may I assist you?"; "Do you need help with something?"; "What would you like me to do for you?" etc. This will ensure that the bot has multiple options to present the same inquiry in different ways, thus providing additional variety and flexibility when engaging with users.

Prompts can also be used as part of training datasets when teaching new concepts or skills to an AI model. For instance, if you want your chatbot to understand FAQ requests about product knowledge, then you could use prompt phrases like "what is X?" or "tell me about Y" as part of your training dataset so that the model learns how to recognize these types of questions and respond appropriately.

Technique for Prompt Writing

The best technique for writing a prompt for ChatGPT depends on the specific task or goal you want to achieve with the model. However, here are some general tips and best practices to keep in mind:

1. Be clear and specific: Clearly state what you want the model to do and what kind of output you expect. Avoid using overly complex or ambiguous language, and provide enough context for the model to understand what you're asking for.
2. Use context: Provide the model with enough context to understand the task at hand. For example, if you're asking the model to generate a response to a customer's question, provide the question and any relevant background information.
3. Be concise: Keep your prompts as short and to the point as possible. The model is more likely to generate accurate and coherent responses when it has less information to process.
4. Test and refine: Once you've written your prompt, test it with the model and see how it performs. If the output is not what you were expecting, refine your prompt accordingly.
5. Use examples: Provide examples of the kind of output you're expecting to help guide the model. For example, if you're asking the model to generate a conversation, provide examples of previous conversations that were similar in nature.

Overall, the key to writing effective prompts for ChatGPT is to be clear, concise and consistent in your writing and to provide the model with enough context to understand the task at hand.

Best Practices for Utilizing Prompts in ChatGPT

When utilizing prompts within your conversational AI models built on ChatGPT there are some important best practices to keep in mind:

- Keep prompts short and concise – Too much detail can lead to confusion or make conversations overly complicated.
- Include helpful phrases within each response template – Phrases like "Let me know if there is anything else I can help with?" encourage users to continue the dialogue which helps build trust and ultimately leads to better user experiences overall.
- Avoid including too many options – Too many choices can lead users down rabbit holes instead of helping them find solutions more quickly.

By following these best practices and leveraging prompts within your ChatGPT applications, you can create smoother interactions that result in better outcomes for both users and developers alike!

Top 20 Ways That ChatGPT is Being Used

1) Generating human-like text for chatbots and virtual assistants

Chatbots and virtual assistants are computer programs that are designed to simulate human conversation. They are becoming increasingly popular in a variety of industries, including customer service, e-commerce, and entertainment. The goal of these programs is to provide a seamless and natural conversational experience for users.

The use of ChatGPT in chatbot and virtual assistant development is based on its ability to generate human-like text. By training ChatGPT on a large dataset of human conversation, the model is able to understand and replicate the nuances of human language. This allows chatbots and virtual assistants powered by ChatGPT to respond to user inputs in a way that feels natural and human-like.

One of the key benefits of using ChatGPT for chatbot and virtual assistant development is its ability to handle a wide range of inputs. ChatGPT is able to understand and respond to a variety of different sentence structures and language patterns. This allows the chatbot or virtual assistant to handle a wide range of user inputs, and to provide relevant and accurate responses.

Another advantage of using ChatGPT for chatbot and virtual assistant development is its ability to generate personalized responses. By training ChatGPT on a dataset of user data, it is possible to create a chatbot or virtual assistant that is able to provide personalized responses based on the user's preferences and history. For example, a chatbot that is trained on a dataset of customer service interactions will be able to provide personalized responses to customer inquiries, based on their past interactions with the company.

ChatGPT has also been used to generate human-like text in order to improve the performance of existing chatbots and virtual assistants. By fine-tuning ChatGPT on a dataset of user interactions, it is possible to improve the accuracy and fluency of the chatbot's responses. This can lead to a more seamless and natural conversational experience for users.

One of the most interesting aspects of the usage of ChatGPT in chatbot and virtual assistant is its ability to generate open-ended responses. The model can generate a variety of different responses to a single input, which allows for a more dynamic and engaging conversational experience. This can be especially useful in the context of customer service, where a chatbot needs to be able to handle a wide range of user inputs and provide relevant and accurate responses.

However, it is worth noting that using ChatGPT for chatbot and virtual assistant development does have its limitations. One of the main challenges is that the model is only as good as the data it is trained on. Therefore, if the dataset used to train ChatGPT is not diverse or representative of the users it will be interacting with, the chatbot or virtual assistant may not be able to provide accurate or relevant responses.

Another limitation is that ChatGPT is not capable of understanding the context of the conversation, it can generate text that sounds human-like but it can't understand the intent or the meaning behind the text. It is necessary to implement other technologies like NLP to understand the context of the conversation.

Example Prompts and Output

Prompt: "Hello, how can I help you today?"
Output: "I'm looking for information about the return policy for a product I recently purchased."

Prompt: "What is the weather like today?"
Output: "It's currently sunny and 75 degrees in New York City."
Prompt: "Can you recommend a good Italian restaurant in the city?" Output: "I would recommend trying out Lombardi's Pizza, it's been voted the best pizza in New York City multiple times."
Prompt: "What are the top news headlines today?" Output: "1. Stock markets continue to climb despite economic uncertainty. 2. Protests erupt in major cities over police brutality. 3. Scientists make breakthrough in cancer research."
Prompt: "What is the definition of Machine Learning?" Output: "Machine Learning is a method of data analysis that automates analytical model building. It is a branch of artificial intelligence based on the idea that systems can learn from data, identify patterns and make decisions with minimal human intervention."
These examples show how ChatGPT can be used to generate human-like text in response to various prompts for chatbots and virtual assistants. The output generated by the model can be fine-tuned and customized based on the specific use case and application.

2. Answering Questions and Providing Information

One of the most popular applications of ChatGPT is in answering questions and providing information.

The ability to answer questions and provide information is a crucial aspect of many natural language processing (NLP) tasks, such as question answering, information retrieval, and knowledge-based systems. These tasks require a deep understanding of the meaning of text, as well as the ability to generate natural and accurate responses.

ChatGPT is well-suited to these tasks because of its ability to generate human-like text. By training ChatGPT on a large dataset of text, the model is able to understand the meaning and context of the text and generate accurate and relevant responses to questions.

One of the key benefits of using ChatGPT for question answering and information retrieval is its ability to handle a wide range of inputs. ChatGPT is able to understand and respond to a variety of different sentence structures and language patterns, which allows it to handle a wide range of user inputs. This makes it ideal for use in knowledge-based systems and other applications that require the ability to understand and respond to a wide range of user inputs.

Another advantage of using ChatGPT for question answering and information retrieval is its ability to generate personalized responses. By fine-tuning ChatGPT on a dataset of user interactions, it is possible to create a model that is able to provide personalized responses based on the user's preferences and history. This can be especially useful in applications such as customer service, where a chatbot needs to be able to provide relevant and accurate responses based on the user's past interactions.

ChatGPT has also been used to improve the performance of existing question answering and information retrieval systems. By fine-tuning ChatGPT on a dataset of user interactions, it is possible to improve the accuracy and fluency of the responses generated by the system. This can lead to a more seamless and natural user experience, which is particularly important in applications such as customer service and e-commerce.

Examples Prompts and Output

Prompt: "What is the capital of France?"
Output: "The capital of France is Paris."

Prompt: "When was the American Civil War?"
Output: "The American Civil War was fought between 1861 and 1865."
Prompt: "What is the boiling point of water in Celsius?" Output: "The boiling point of water in Celsius is 100 degrees."
Prompt: "What is the largest planet in our solar system?" Output: "The largest planet in our solar system is Jupiter."
Prompt: "How many states are there in the United States of America?" Output: "There are 50 states in the United States of America."
These examples show how ChatGPT can be used to answer questions and provide information in a concise and accurate manner. The model can be fine-tuned to provide more detailed information or context as needed. Additionally, it can be used as a tool to handle a variety of questions and provide relevant and accurate answers in real time.

3. Generating content such as articles, stories, and product descriptions

One of the most popular applications of ChatGPT is in generating content such as articles, stories, and product descriptions.

The ability to generate text is a crucial aspect of many natural language processing (NLP) tasks, such as text generation, content creation, and language translation. These tasks require a deep understanding of the meaning of text, as well as the ability to generate natural and accurate text.

ChatGPT has also been used to improve the performance of existing content generation systems. By fine-tuning ChatGPT on a dataset of user interactions, it is possible to improve the accuracy and fluency of the text generated by the system. This can lead to a more seamless and natural user experience, which is particularly important in applications such as content creation and language translation.

Another interesting aspect of the usage of ChatGPT in content generation is its ability to generate open-ended responses. The model can generate a variety of different responses to a single input, which allows for a more dynamic and engaging user experience. This can be especially useful in the context of creative writing and storytelling, where a model needs to be able to generate a wide range of different stories and narratives.

Example Prompts and Output

Prompt: "Write a product description for a new electric car"

Output:

Introducing the all-new electric car from XYZ Motors – the ultimate in eco-friendly transportation. With its sleek and aerodynamic design, this car is not only stylish but also energy-efficient. The car is equipped with a powerful electric motor that delivers instant torque and smooth acceleration. It also has a range of up to 300 miles on a single charge, making it perfect for long-distance road trips. The car also features advanced safety and driver-assist technologies, such as lane departure warning and automatic emergency braking, to provide you with a safe and comfortable driving experience.

Prompt: "Write a short story about a time traveler"

Output:
It was a normal Wednesday afternoon when Jack stumbled upon the time machine. It was tucked away in the back corner of his uncle's dusty old attic, covered in cobwebs and forgotten for years. Jack had always been fascinated by the concept of time travel, and now he finally had the chance to make it a reality. He quickly set the dials and hit the button, and in a flash, he was hurtling through time.

At first, everything was a blur. He saw flashes of different eras and civilizations, each one more incredible than the last. He landed in ancient Egypt, where he walked among the pyramids and marveled at the engineering feats of the pharaohs. He visited the court of King Arthur, where he witnessed the legendary sword in the stone ceremony. He even got to meet some of the great minds of history, such as Leonardo da Vinci and Albert Einstein.

But as the days turned into weeks and the weeks turned into months, Jack realized that he had been away from home for too long. He missed his family, his friends, and the life he had left behind. He quickly set the dials and hit the button, and soon he was back in his uncle's attic, where he had started his journey.

He knew that he couldn't stay there forever, he had to go back to his normal life, but he was changed forever, he had seen and lived things that most people could only dream of.

Prompt: "Write an article about the benefits of meditation"

Output:
Meditation is a practice that has been used for thousands of years to promote mental and physical well-being. It involves sitting in a quiet place, focusing on your breath, and clearing your mind of distracting thoughts.

While it may seem simple, meditation can have a profound impact on your overall health and well-being.

One of the most well-known benefits of meditation is its ability to reduce stress and anxiety. When you meditate, you focus on your breath and let go of any worries or negative thoughts. This helps to calm your mind and reduce feelings of stress and anxiety.

Meditation also has a positive impact on your physical health. It has been shown to lower blood pressure, improve heart health, and reduce chronic pain. Additionally, it can also improve sleep, boost the immune system, and increase feelings of well-being.

Meditation can also help you to improve your focus and concentration. By regularly practicing meditation, you can train your mind to focus on the present moment, which can help you to be more productive and efficient in your daily life.

Finally, meditation can help you to cultivate a sense of inner peace and contentment. By regularly practicing meditation, you can develop a deeper understanding of yourself and your place in the world, and find a sense of inner peace that is not dependent on external circumstances.

4. Summarizing and analyzing text

The ability to summarize and analyze text is a crucial aspect of many natural language processing (NLP) tasks, such as text summarization, sentiment analysis, and topic modeling.

One advantage of using ChatGPT for text summarization is its ability to generate personalized summaries. By fine-tuning ChatGPT on a dataset of user interactions, it is possible to create a model that is able to generate summaries that are personalized to the user's preferences and history. This can be especially useful in applications such as news summarization, where a model needs to be able to generate summaries that are personalized to the user's interests.

ChatGPT has also been used to improve the performance of existing text summarization systems. By fine-tuning ChatGPT on a dataset of user interactions, it is possible to improve the accuracy and fluency of the summaries generated by the system. This can lead to a more seamless and natural user experience, which is particularly important in applications such as news summarization and document summarization.

One of the most interesting aspects of the usage of ChatGPT in text summarization is its ability to generate open-ended summaries. The model can generate a variety of different summaries for a single input, which allows for a more dynamic and engaging user experience. This can be especially useful in the context of news summarization, where a model needs to be able to generate a wide range of different summaries for a single news article.

By training ChatGPT on a large dataset of text, it is possible to create systems that are able to generate accurate and relevant summaries. The ability to handle a wide range of inputs, generate personalized summaries and improve the performance of existing summarization systems make ChatGPT a great tool for summarizing and analyzing text.

Example Prompts and Output

Prompt: "Please summarize this article about the economic impact of the COVID-19 pandemic" Article: "The COVID-19 pandemic has had a devastating impact on the global economy. Businesses have had to close their doors and millions of people have lost their jobs. The stock market has also taken a hit, with many companies seeing their stock prices plummet. The International Monetary Fund has predicted that the global economy will shrink by 4.4% in 2020. Governments around the world have had to take action to try and mitigate the damage, with many implementing stimulus packages to help businesses and individuals. Experts are warning that the recovery may be slow and difficult, with some predicting that it could take years for the global economy to fully recover."

Output: "The article discusses the severe economic impact of the COVID-19 pandemic, with businesses shutting down and millions losing jobs. The stock market has also been affected. The International Monetary Fund predicts a 4.4% shrink of the global economy in 2020. Governments are implementing stimulus packages to help mitigate the damage, but experts warn that the recovery could be slow and difficult, taking years to fully recover."

Prompt: "Please analyze the sentiment of this tweet: "I am so excited to finally see the new Star Wars movie!"

Tweet: "I am so excited to finally see the new Star Wars movie!"

Output: "The sentiment of this tweet is positive. The language used in the tweet such as "excited" and "finally" indicate that the person is looking forward to the event and has been waiting for it."

These examples show how ChatGPT can be used to summarize and analyze text, for instance, it can be used to extract the main ideas from an article or to identify the sentiment of a tweet. The model can be fine-tuned to adapt to different types of texts, and to identify specific entities or concepts. Additionally, it can be used to extract insights and trends from large volumes of unstructured data.

5. Translating text from one language to another

Machine translation is the process of using computer algorithms to automatically translate text from one language to another. It is a complex task that requires a deep understanding of the meaning and context of the text, as well as the ability to generate natural and accurate translations.

ChatGPT is well-suited to the task of machine translation because of its ability to generate human-like text. By training ChatGPT on a large dataset of parallel text, the model is able to understand the meaning and context of the text in one language and generate accurate and relevant translations in the target language.

ChatGPT is able to understand and respond to a variety of different sentence structures and language patterns, which allows it to handle a wide range of text inputs. This makes it ideal for use in machine translation tasks across multiple languages and domains.

Another advantage of using ChatGPT for machine translation is its ability to generate translations that are close to human-like. The model is able to understand the nuances and subtleties of the language, which allows it to generate translations that are more fluent and natural-sounding. This is especially important in applications such as customer service, where the goal is to provide translations that are as close to human-generated as possible.

Example Prompts and Output

Prompt: "Please translate this sentence from Spanish to English: ¿Cómo estás?"
Sentence: "¿Cómo estás?"

Output: "How are you?"

Prompt: "Please translate this sentence from French to German: Je suis fatigué"
Sentence: "Je suis fatigué"

Output: "Ich bin müde"

Prompt: "Please translate this sentence from Chinese to English: 我爱你"

Sentence: "我爱你"

Output: "I love you"

These examples demonstrate how ChatGPT can be used to translate text from one language to another. However, it's important to note that while GPT-3 has a large language model, it is not specifically designed to translate text. There are specialized neural machine translation models that are more accurate and efficient. Additionally, the translations may not be perfect, as the model may not understand the context, grammar, and idiomatic expressions of the text.

6. Generating code and programming assistance

ChatGPT is a powerful tool for generating code and providing programming assistance. Its ability to understand the meaning and context of text, and its ability to generate human-like text make it well-suited for this task. By training ChatGPT on a large dataset of code and programming documentation, the model can understand the syntax and structure of code, and generate accurate and relevant code snippets.

ChatGPT ideal for use in code generation tasks across multiple languages and frameworks, such as Python, Java, C++ and more.

The model is able to understand the nuances and subtleties of the code, which allows it to generate code that is more readable, maintainable, and efficient. This is especially important in applications such as programming education, where the goal is to provide code examples that are as close to human-generated as possible.

ChatGPT has also been used to improve the performance of existing code generation systems. By fine-tuning ChatGPT on a dataset of code snippets, it is possible to improve the accuracy and fluency of the code generated by the system. This can lead to a more seamless and natural user experience, which is particularly important in applications such as programming education and code-assistant tools.

One of the most interesting aspects of using ChatGPT for code generation is its ability to generate code snippets that match specific requirements. For instance, given a specific problem or task, the model can generate code that can solve the problem or accomplish the task. This can be especially useful in the context of programming education, where students are taught how to write code to solve specific problems.

Additionally, ChatGPT can be used for tasks such as code completion, where it can generate missing parts of code, and code correction, where it can suggest modifications to existing code to make it more efficient or correct errors. This can be extremely useful for developers, as it can save time and resources.

In conclusion, ChatGPT is a powerful tool for generating code and providing programming assistance. Its ability to handle a wide range of programming languages and frameworks, generate human-like code and improve existing code generation systems make it a valuable tool for programming education and code-assistant tools. It can be used for tasks such as code completion, code correction and even generating code that matches specific requirements which can save time and resources.

Example Prompts and Output

Prompt: "Write a Python function to calculate the area of a circle with a given radius"
Output:

```
def circle_area(radius): return 3.14 * (radius ** 2)
```

Prompt: "How do I implement a bubble sort algorithm in Java?"

Output:
```
public static void bubbleSort(int[] arr) {
  int n = arr.length;
  for (int i = 0; i < n-1; i++)
    for (int j = 0; j < n-i-1; j++)
      if (arr[j] > arr[j+1]) {
        int temp = arr[j];
        arr[j] = arr[j+1];
        arr[j+1] = temp;
      }
}
```
Prompt: "How can I fix this error: 'TypeError: 'str' object is not callable' in Python?"

Output:
The error message is indicating that you have a variable named "str" in your code that is causing a conflict with the built-in Python str function. To fix this, you can either change the name of the variable or use the "del" keyword to remove the variable before calling the str function.

These examples demonstrate how ChatGPT can be used to generate code and provide programming assistance. It can be used to generate code snippets in different programming languages, answer programming questions, and troubleshoot code errors. However, it's important to note that the generated code may not be perfect, as the model may not understand the specific requirements or constraints of the task, and it may require human revision.

7. Personalizing and customizing content

One of the most popular applications of ChatGPT for personalization and customization of content is in the field of e-commerce. Online retailers are using ChatGPT to generate product descriptions that are tailored to the preferences and interests of individual users. For example, an online clothing retailer may use ChatGPT to generate product descriptions for a specific item of clothing, such as a pair of jeans. By training ChatGPT on a dataset of product descriptions for similar items of clothing, the model is able to understand the characteristics and features of the jeans and generate a personalized product description that is tailored to the preferences of the user.

Another example of how ChatGPT is being used for personalization and customization of content is in the field of news. News organizations are using ChatGPT to generate personalized news summaries for individual users. For example, a news organization may use ChatGPT to generate a personalized news summary for a specific user, based on their interests and reading history. By fine-tuning ChatGPT on a dataset of user interactions, the model is able to understand the user's preferences and generate a personalized news summary that is tailored to the user's interests. In the field of social media, ChatGPT is being used to generate personalized responses to user's comments and messages. For example, a social media platform may use ChatGPT to generate personalized responses to user comments on a specific post. By training ChatGPT on a dataset of comments and responses, the model is able to understand the context of the comment and generate a personalized response that is tailored to the user's comment.

ChatGPT is also being used in the field of marketing. Companies are using ChatGPT to generate personalized marketing messages and advertisements that are tailored to the preferences and interests of individual users. For example, a company may use ChatGPT to generate personalized email marketing messages for a specific user, based on their browsing and purchase history. By fine-tuning ChatGPT on a dataset of user interactions, the model is able to understand the user's preferences and generate a personalized marketing message that is tailored to the user's interests.

In addition to these examples, ChatGPT is also being used to generate personalized content across a wide range of other domains, such as education, entertainment, and customer service. In all of these applications, ChatGPT is able to generate personalized content that is tailored to the preferences and interests of individual users, which leads to a more engaging and personalized user experience.

Example Prompts and Output

Prompt: "Please write a personalized email message to John, thanking him for his business and offering him a special promotion."

Output:
"Dear John,

I wanted to take a moment to personally thank you for your continued business with us. Your loyalty and support mean a lot to us and we truly appreciate it.
As a token of our gratitude, we would like to offer you a special promotion. For a limited time, we are offering 15% off your next purchase.
We hope that this offer will give you an even better experience with our company.

Thank you again for your support, and we look forward to serving you again in the near future.

Sincerely,
[Your Name]"

Prompt: "Please write a customized message for a birthday card"

Output:
"Happy birthday my dear [Name],

Wishing you all the best on your special day! May all your dreams and wishes come true.

You are an amazing person and I am so grateful to have you in my life. I hope that this birthday is just the beginning of a year filled with happiness, love, and success.

Enjoy your day and celebrate it to the fullest!

With love,
[Your Name]"

These examples demonstrate how ChatGPT can be used to personalize and customize content, such as writing personalized emails and customized messages for different occasions. The model can be fine-tuned to adapt to different styles and tone of voice, and to include specific information such as name, date and other details. Additionally, It can be used to generate personalized content for different audiences and situations.

8. Generating creative writing prompts and exercises

One of the most popular applications of ChatGPT for generating creative writing prompts and exercises is in the field of education. Many writing teachers are using ChatGPT to generate writing prompts and exercises that are tailored to the interests and abilities of their students. For example, a writing teacher may use ChatGPT to generate a writing prompt for a specific student, based on the student's interests and writing abilities. By fine-tuning ChatGPT on a dataset of student writing samples, the model is able to understand the student's writing style and generate a writing prompt that is tailored to the student's interests and abilities.

Another example of how ChatGPT is being used for generating creative writing prompts and exercises is in the field of self-improvement. Many writing coaches and authors are using ChatGPT to generate writing prompts and exercises that are designed to help writers improve their skills. For example, a writing coach may use ChatGPT to generate a writing exercise that is designed to help a writer improve their descriptive writing skills. By fine-tuning ChatGPT on a dataset of writing samples, the model is able to understand the writer's needs and generate a writing exercise that is tailored to the writer's skill level.

In the field of entertainment, ChatGPT is being used to generate creative writing prompts for storytellers and writers. For example, a script writer may use ChatGPT to generate a writing prompt for a specific scene of a movie or a TV show. By fine-tuning ChatGPT on a dataset of script writing, the model is able to understand the context of the scene and generate a writing prompt that is tailored to the scene.

In the field of creative writing, ChatGPT is being used by writers to generate ideas and prompts for their stories, novels, and poetry. By fine-tuning ChatGPT on a dataset of creative writing, the model is able to understand the writing style of the writer and generate ideas and prompts that align with the writer's style. This can be particularly helpful for writers who are experiencing writer's block and need inspiration to continue their work.

In addition to these examples, ChatGPT is also being used to generate creative writing prompts and exercises across a wide range of other domains, such as journalism, marketing, and advertising. In all of these applications, ChatGPT is able to generate creative writing prompts and exercises that are tailored to the interests and abilities of individual users, which leads to a more engaging and personalized writing experience.

Example Prompts and Output

Prompt: "Please generate a creative writing prompt for a short story about a person who discovers a mysterious object in their backyard"

Output: "Write a short story about a person who discovers a mysterious, ancient artifact buried deep in their backyard. As they begin to uncover its secrets, they start to realize the incredible power it holds and the impact it will have on their life and the lives of those around them."

Prompt: "Please generate an exercise for a poetry class about the theme of love"

Output: "For this exercise, write a poem about the theme of love. Imagine you are in a long distance relationship, write a letter to your loved one expressing your feelings, thoughts, and longing. Use sensory details and imagery to describe the emotions and distance that separates you both."

These examples demonstrate how ChatGPT can be used to generate creative writing prompts and exercises. The model can be fine-tuned to generate prompts for different genres and styles, and to include specific themes, characters, and settings. Additionally, it can be used to generate exercises for different writing levels, from beginner to advanced. It's important to note that while GPT-3 can generate creative prompts and exercises, the quality and originality of the final writing will depend on the writer's skill and imagination.

9. Generating audio and video scripts

ChatGPT is for ideal for use in script generation tasks across multiple domains, such as film, television, and video games.

For example, in the field of film and television, ChatGPT has been used to generate scripts for upcoming movies and TV shows. By fine-tuning ChatGPT on a dataset of scriptwriting, the model can understand the plot, characters, and tone of the movie or TV show, and generate a script that aligns with those elements. This can save a lot of time for scriptwriters and production companies, as they can quickly generate a script that aligns with their vision for the project.

In the field of video games, ChatGPT has been used to generate dialogue and conversations between NPCs (non-player characters) and characters. By fine-tuning ChatGPT on a dataset of video game dialogue, the model is able to understand the tone, plot, and characters in the game, and generate dialogue that aligns with those elements. This can lead to a more immersive and engaging gaming experience for players.

Another application of ChatGPT in audio and video script generation is in the field of podcasting. Podcast creators have been using ChatGPT to generate scripts for their episodes. By fine-tuning ChatGPT on a dataset of podcast episodes, the model can understand the tone, style, and format of the podcast, and generate a script that aligns with those elements. This can save a lot of time for podcast creators, as they can quickly generate a script that aligns with their vision for the episode.

ChatGPT has also been used in the field of radio and audio production. By fine-tuning ChatGPT on a dataset of radio and audio scripts, the model can understand the tone, style and format of the production, and generate a script that aligns with those elements. This can save a lot of time for radio and audio producers, as they can quickly generate a script that aligns with their vision for the production.

ChatGPT is also being used in the field of advertising, to generate scripts for commercials and advertisements that are tailored to the preferences and interests of individual users. By fine-tuning ChatGPT on a dataset of advertising scripts, the model is able to understand the tone, style, and format of the advertisement, and generate a script that aligns with those elements. This can lead to a more engaging and effective advertising experience for users.

Example Prompts and Output

Prompt: "Please write a script for a 30-second commercial for a new car brand"

Output:

Opening shot of a sleek, new car driving down a winding road.

Narrator: "Introducing the all-new X1, the ultimate driving machine."

Cut to close-up of car's exterior features. Narrator: "Featuring a powerful engine, advanced safety technologies, and a design that turns heads."

Cut to interior shot of car, panning over the dashboard and controls.

Narrator: "Experience the thrill of the open road like never before."

Cut to people of different ages and backgrounds driving and enjoying the car.

Narrator: "Get behind the wheel of the X1 today and see for yourself why it's the car of the future."

Closing shot of car driving off into the sunset.

Narrator: "X1, drive one home."

Prompt: "Please write a script for a 5-minute video on how to plant a vegetable garden"

Output:

Opening shot of a backyard with a small patch of barren land.

Narrator: "Are you ready to start your own vegetable garden? Well, you've come to the right place. In this video, we're going to show you how to plant your very own vegetable garden in just 5 minutes."

Cut to a person preparing the soil by removing rocks and debris.

Narrator: "First, you'll need to prepare the soil. Remove any rocks or debris and make sure the soil is loose and well-draining."

Cut to person planting the seeds.

Narrator: "Next, it's time to plant your seeds or seedlings. Follow the instructions on the packet for the correct planting depth and spacing."

Cut to person watering the plants.

Narrator: "Don't forget to water your new garden regularly, making sure the soil stays moist but not waterlogged."

Cut to time-lapse of the garden growing.

Narrator: "With a little bit of patience and care, you'll soon be reaping the rewards of your hard work."

Closing shot of a person picking and eating ripe vegetables from the garden.

Narrator: "Happy gardening!"
These examples demonstrate how ChatGPT can be used to generate scripts for audio and video content. The model can be fine-tuned to

adapt to different types of audio and video content, such as commercials, tutorials, and explainer videos. It is important to note that while GPT-3 can generate script, the final video or audio content will depend on the director and the production team, who will be responsible for bringing the script to life.

10. Generating legal and financial documents

ChatGPT has been used to generate legal documents such as contracts, agreements, and legal briefs. By fine-tuning ChatGPT on a dataset of legal documents, the model can understand the legal jargon and formatting of the documents, and generate a document that aligns with those elements. This can save a lot of time for lawyers, as they can quickly generate a document that meets the legal requirements without having to manually write each document.

In the field of finance, ChatGPT has been used to generate financial documents such as financial statements, reports, and budgets. By fine-tuning ChatGPT on a dataset of financial documents, the model can understand the financial jargon and formatting of the documents, and generate a document that aligns with those elements. This can save a lot of time for financial analysts, accountants, and other financial professionals, as they can quickly generate a document that meets the financial requirements without having to manually write each document.

Another application of ChatGPT in legal and financial document generation is in the field of compliance. Many companies are using ChatGPT to generate compliance reports and documents such as KYC (know your customer) and AML (anti-money laundering) documentation. By fine-tuning ChatGPT on a dataset of compliance documents, the model can understand the formatting and legal requirements of the document, and generate a document that aligns with those elements. This can save a lot of time for compliance professionals, as they can quickly generate a document that meets the regulatory requirements without having to manually write each document.

ChatGPT has also been used in the field of insurance, to generate insurance policies and claims forms that are tailored to the preferences and interests of individual users. By fine-tuning ChatGPT on a dataset of insurance documents, the model is able to understand the formatting and legal requirements of the document, and generate a document that aligns with those elements. This can lead to a more efficient and accurate process for creating insurance policies and claims forms.

ChatGPT is being used in the field of banking, to generate loan agreements and financial reports that are tailored to the preferences and interests of individual customers. By fine-tuning ChatGPT on a dataset of banking documents, the model is able to understand the formatting and legal requirements of the document, and generate a document that aligns with those elements. This can lead to a more efficient and accurate process for creating loan agreements and financial reports, and provide a better customer experience as the documents are tailored to their specific needs. Additionally, this technology can help the banks to minimize the human errors and improve the speed of the process.

Example Prompts and Output

Prompt: "Please generate a non-disclosure agreement for a software development project."

Output: "NON-DISCLOSURE AGREEMENT

This Non-Disclosure Agreement (the "Agreement") is entered into as of [date] by and between [Disclosing Party] (the "Disclosing Party") and [Receiving Party] (the "Receiving Party").

Purpose of Agreement. The Disclosing Party desires to disclose certain proprietary and confidential information to the Receiving Party, and the Receiving Party desires to receive and protect such information from unauthorized use and disclosure.

Definition of Confidential Information. For purposes of this Agreement, "Confidential Information" shall include all information or material that has or could have commercial value or other utility in the business in which Disclosing Party is engaged. If the Confidential Information is in written form, the Disclosing Party shall label or stamp the materials with the word "Confidential" or some similar warning. If Confidential Information is transmitted orally, the Disclosing Party shall promptly provide writing indicating that such oral communication constituted Confidential Information.

Exclusions from Confidential Information. Receiving Party's obligations under this Agreement do not extend to information that is: (a) publicly known at the time of disclosure or subsequently becomes publicly known through no fault of the Receiving Party; (b) discovered or created by the Receiving Party before disclosure by Disclosing Party; (c) learned by the Receiving Party through legitimate means other than from Disclosing Party or Disclosing Party's representatives; or (d) is disclosed by Receiving Party with Disclosing Party's prior written approval.

Obligations of Receiving Party. Receiving Party shall hold and maintain the Confidential Information in strictest confidence for the sole and exclusive benefit of the Disclosing Party. Receiving Party shall carefully restrict access to Confidential Information to employees, contractors and third parties as is reasonably required and shall require those persons to sign nondisclosure restrictions at least as protective as those in this Agreement.

Time Periods. The nondisclosure provisions of this Agreement shall survive the termination of this Agreement and Receiving Party's duty to hold Confidential Information in confidence shall remain in effect until the Confidential Information no longer qualifies as a trade secret or until Disclosing Party sends written notice releasing Receiving Party from this Agreement, whichever occurs first.

Relationships. Nothing contained in this Agreement shall be deemed to constitute either party a partner, joint venture or employee of the other party for any purpose.

Severability. If a court finds any provision of this Agreement invalid or unenforceable, the remainder of this Agreement shall be interpreted so as best to affect the intent of the parties.

Integration. This Agreement expresses the complete understanding of the parties regarding its subject matter and supersedes all prior proposals, agreements, representations, and understandings. This Agreement may not be amended except in writing signed by both parties.

Waiver. The failure to exercise any right provided in this Agreement shall not be a waiver of prior or subsequent rights.
IN WITNESS WHEREOF, the parties have executed this Agreement through their authorized representatives.

Disclosing Party: [Name and Title]

Receiving Party: [Name and Title]"

Prompt: "Please generate a legal document for a loan agreement between two parties."

Output: "LOAN AGREEMENT

This Loan Agreement (the "Agreement") is made and entered into as of [date], by and between [Lender Name] (the "Lender") and [Borrower Name] (the "Borrower").

Purpose of Loan. The Lender agrees to loan the Borrower the sum of [Loan Amount] (the "Loan"), on the terms and conditions set forth in this Agreement.

Repayment of Loan. The Borrower shall repay the Loan to the Lender in [Number of Payments] equal payments of [Payment Amount] each, beginning on [First Payment Date] and continuing on the [Repayment Schedule] thereafter, until the Loan is fully repaid.

Interest. The Loan shall accrue interest at the rate of [Interest Rate]% per annum, calculated on the unpaid balance of the Loan.

Collateral. The Borrower shall pledge [Collateral Description] as collateral for the Loan. In the event of default, the Lender shall have the right to foreclose on the collateral.

Default. The Borrower shall be in default under this Agreement in the event of any material breach of any provision of this Agreement, including the failure to make any payment when due.

Remedies. In the event of default, the Lender shall have the right to declare the entire unpaid balance of the Loan immediately due and payable, and to exercise any other rights and remedies as provided by law.

Governing Law. This Agreement shall be governed by and construed in accordance with the laws of the state of [Governing Law].

Entire Agreement. This Agreement constitutes the entire agreement between the parties with respect to the subject matter hereof and supersedes all prior and contemporaneous agreements and understandings, whether oral or written.

Amendment. This Agreement may not be amended or modified except in writing signed by both parties.

Waiver. The failure to exercise any right provided in this Agreement shall not be a waiver of prior or subsequent rights.

IN WITNESS WHEREOF, the parties have executed this Agreement through their authorized representatives.

Lender: [Name and Title]

Borrower: [Name and Title]

Date: [Date Signed]

It is important to note that these documents are just examples and may not be suitable for all situations and should be reviewed and modified by a licensed attorney to ensure they are legally compliant and appropriate for the specific situation.

11. Poetry, Lyrics and Song Title Generation

ChatGPT's ability to understand and generate natural language text makes it a powerful tool for poetry, lyrics and song title generation.

One example of ChatGPT being used to generate poetry is the "Poet Assistant" application, which allows users to input a theme or keyword and generates a poem based on that input. For example, inputting the theme "love" might generate a poem that reads:

"Love is a rose, delicate and fair
With petals soft and fragrant air
It blossoms in the heart of spring
And makes the world a brighter thing"

ChatGPT has also been used to generate song lyrics. One example is the application "LyricAI" which allows users to input a theme or artist and generates song lyrics based on that input. For example, inputting the artist "Bob Dylan" might generate lyrics that read:

"Oh the times, they are a-changin'
The leaves fall from the trees
But my love for you will never fade
Like the colors of the leaves"

Another way ChatGPT is being used in the music industry is by generating song titles.

One example is "Song Title Generator", which allows users to input a theme or genre and generates a song title based on that input. For example, inputting the theme "heartbreak" might generate the song title "Broken Heart Symphony".

ChatGPT's ability to understand and generate natural language text makes it a powerful tool for creative applications such as poetry, lyrics, and song title generation. These examples show how ChatGPT can be used to generate a wide range of creative content, from poems and song lyrics to song titles.

However, it's important to note that while ChatGPT can generate coherent and sometimes even poetic or catchy text, it is not a replacement for human creativity. The output generated by the model may require human editing and refinement to become fully polished and engaging piece of art.

Additionally, it's important to consider ethical and legal issues when using AI-generated content, such as ensuring proper attribution, obtaining permission, and respecting copyright laws.

12. Generating jokes and humor

One of the ways that ChatGPT is being used is in the generation of jokes and humor.

One of the key advantages of using ChatGPT for joke generation is its ability to understand the context and intent behind a prompt. This allows it to generate jokes that are relevant and appropriate for a given situation. For example, a prompt such as "generate a dad joke" will result in a joke that follows the structure and style of a typical dad joke, while a prompt such as "generate a political joke" will result in a joke that is more pointed and satirical.

Another advantage of using ChatGPT for joke generation is its ability to generate a wide variety of jokes. Since it has been trained on a large amount of text data, it has a deep understanding of different types of jokes, from puns to one-liners to observational humor. This means that it can generate jokes that will appeal to a wide range of audiences and tastes.

One popular use case for ChatGPT in generating jokes is in the creation of social media content. Companies, brands, and influencers can use ChatGPT to generate funny, engaging posts that will help to increase engagement and reach on their social media platforms. For example, a food company might use ChatGPT to generate jokes and puns related to their products, while a fashion brand might use it to generate jokes about the latest trends.

Another use case for ChatGPT in generating jokes is in the entertainment industry. ChatGPT can be used to generate script ideas, punchlines, and even entire skits. This can save a lot of time for writers and comedians and can also open up new possibilities for creative expression.

While ChatGPT is an incredibly powerful tool for joke generation, it is important to note that it is not perfect. Like any AI model, it is only as good as the data it has been trained on. This means that it may generate jokes that are insensitive, offensive, or otherwise inappropriate. Therefore, it is important to always review the output of ChatGPT and make sure that it aligns with your values and goals.

Example Prompts and Output

Prompt: "Generate a dad joke"
Output: "Why don't scientists trust atoms? Because they make up everything"
Prompt: "Generate a political joke"
Output: "Why did the politician cross the road? To get away from the truth"
Prompt: "Generate a pun about books"
Output: "Why did the book look sad? Because its cover was too long"
Prompt: "Generate a one-liner about the weather"
Output: "I don't trust the weatherman, but if he says it's going to rain, I bring an umbrella."

13. Generating product review and feedback

One of the key advantages of using ChatGPT for product review generation is its ability to understand the context and intent behind a prompt. This allows it to generate reviews that are relevant and appropriate for a given product. For example, a prompt such as "generate a product review for a new smartphone" will result in a review that covers key features and specifications of the device, while a prompt such as "generate a product review for a skincare product" will result in a review that focuses more on the product's effectiveness and results.

Another advantage of using ChatGPT for product review generation is its ability to generate a wide variety of reviews. Since it has been trained on a large amount of text data, it has a deep understanding of different types of products and the language and tone used to review them. This means that it can generate reviews that will appeal to a wide range of audiences and tastes.

One popular use case for ChatGPT in generating product reviews is in the e-commerce industry. Online retailers can use ChatGPT to generate reviews for their products that can be used on their website or other platforms to provide customers with valuable information about the products. This can save a lot of time for retailers and also increases the quantity of reviews for the products which can help increase sales.

Another use case for ChatGPT in generating product reviews is for companies to monitor the feedback of their products. ChatGPT can be used to generate reviews for products from different sources such as social media, online marketplaces, and more. This can help companies to quickly understand the sentiment of the customers about their products and make necessary changes to improve their products and customer satisfaction.

While ChatGPT is an incredibly powerful tool for product review generation, it is important to note that it is not perfect. Like any AI model, it is only as good as the data it has been trained on. This means that it may generate reviews that are biased, inaccurate, or otherwise inappropriate. Therefore, it is important to always review the output of ChatGPT and make sure that it aligns with your values and goals, and also to cross-check with human reviews.

Example Prompts and Output

Prompt: "Generate a product review for a new laptop"
Output: "I recently purchased this laptop and have been extremely impressed with its performance. The speed of the processor and amount of RAM make multitasking a breeze. The keyboard is comfortable to type on and the touchpad is responsive. The battery life is also impressive. The design is sleek and modern. Overall, I am very satisfied with my purchase and would highly recommend this laptop to anyone in the market for a new one."

Prompt: "Generate a product review for a new pair of running shoes"
Output: "I have been using these running shoes for the past few weeks and I am very happy with my purchase. The shoes are very

comfortable and provide great support for my feet. The soles have good traction and I feel very stable while running. The shoes are also very light which makes running feel effortless. They are also breathable, so my feet stay cool and dry even on longer runs. The design is also modern and stylish. I have been getting many compliments on them. One downside is that they may be a bit expensive for some people. But overall, I think they are worth the investment. If you're in the market for a new pair of running shoes, I highly recommend giving these a try."

14. Generating customer service and support responses

One of the key advantages of using ChatGPT for customer service and support is its ability to understand the context and intent behind a customer's question or issue. This allows it to generate responses that are relevant, accurate and appropriate for a given situation. For example, a prompt such as "generate a response for a customer who is inquiring about a refund" will result in a response that provides clear instructions on how to initiate a refund, while a prompt such as "generate a response for a customer who is reporting a technical issue" will result in a response that acknowledges the issue and provides troubleshooting steps.

Another advantage of using ChatGPT for customer service and support is its ability to generate a wide variety of responses. Since it has been trained on a large amount of text data, it has a deep understanding of different types of customer service scenarios and the language and tone used to respond to them. This means that it can generate responses that will be helpful, empathetic and professional.

One popular use case for ChatGPT in generating customer service and support responses is in the customer service centers of companies. ChatGPT can be used to generate responses for frequently asked questions, providing an efficient way to handle customer inquiries and reduce the workload of customer service representatives. This can save a lot of time for companies and also improve the customer experience by providing quick and accurate responses.

Another use case for ChatGPT in generating customer service and support responses is for chatbots and virtual assistants. ChatGPT can be used to generate responses for chatbot and virtual assistants, providing an automated way to handle customer inquiries and improve the customer experience.

Example Prompts and Output

Prompt: "Generate a response for a customer who is inquiring about a refund"
Output: "I apologize for any inconvenience you may have experienced. To initiate a refund, please fill out the refund form on our website and include your order number and the reason for the refund. Once we receive your request, we will process it within 3-5 business days. If you have any further questions, please let us know."

Prompt: "Generate a response for a customer who is reporting a technical issue"
Output: "Thank you for bringing this to our attention. We apologize for the inconvenience. Can you please provide me with the details of the technical issue and your account information so we can investigate the problem? In the meantime, you can try some basic troubleshooting steps like restarting the device or checking your internet connection. Let me know if you have any further issues and we will do our best to resolve them as soon as possible. We value your feedback and are always looking for ways to improve our products and services. Thank you for bringing this to our attention and for being a valued customer."

15. Generating research papers and academic papers

One of the key advantages of using ChatGPT for research paper and academic paper generation is its ability to understand the context and intent behind a prompt. This allows it to generate papers that are relevant and appropriate for a given topic. For example, a prompt such as "generate a research paper on the effects of climate change on agriculture" will result in a paper that covers the topic in depth, while a prompt such as "generate an academic paper on the history of artificial intelligence" will result in a paper that provides a comprehensive overview of the topic.

Another advantage of using ChatGPT for research paper and academic paper generation is its ability to generate a wide variety of papers. Since it has been trained on a large amount of text data, it has a deep understanding of different research methods, academic style and the language used in writing research and academic papers. This means that it can generate papers that will appeal to a wide range of audiences and tastes, and also will meet the academic standards.

One popular use case for ChatGPT in generating research papers and academic papers is in the field of education. ChatGPT can be used by students and researchers to generate research papers and academic papers, providing a helpful tool for generating ideas, structuring arguments, and organizing information. This can save a lot of time for students and researchers and also open up new possibilities for creative expression.

Another use case for ChatGPT in generating research papers and academic papers is in the field of research and development. ChatGPT can be used by companies and organizations to generate research papers and academic papers on various topics, providing a helpful tool for generating ideas, structuring arguments, and organizing information, and also will save a lot of time and effort for these organizations.

Example Prompts and Output

Prompt: "Generate a research paper on the effects of climate change on agriculture"
Output: "Climate change is having a significant impact on agriculture around the world. Rising temperatures and altered precipitation patterns are affecting crop growth and yields, leading to food insecurity for millions of people. This paper will examine the current state of research on the effects of climate change on agriculture, focusing on key crops and regions. It will also discuss potential mitigation and adaptation strategies for farmers and policymakers.

Prompt: "Generate an academic paper on the history of Artificial Intelligence"
Output: "Artificial intelligence (AI) is a rapidly evolving field with a rich history. This paper will provide an overview of the key milestones and developments in the history of AI, beginning with the earliest ideas and theories in the 1950s and 1960s, and moving through the emergence of expert systems and neural networks in the 1970s and 1980s, to the current state of the art in deep learning and machine learning. It will also examine the impact of AI on society, discussing ethical concerns and potential implications for the future. Throughout the paper, the focus will be on the major figures and groundbreaking research that have shaped the field of AI, and how their work has led to the development of today's technology. Ultimately, this paper aims to provide a comprehensive overview of the history of AI and its impact on the world as we know it."

16. Generating business plans and marketing strategies

One of the key advantages of using ChatGPT for business plan and marketing strategy generation is its ability to understand the context and intent behind a prompt. This allows it to generate plans and strategies that are relevant and appropriate for a given business or market. For example, a prompt such as "generate a business plan for a new e-commerce startup" will result in a plan that outlines the key steps and strategies for building and scaling an e-commerce business, while a prompt such as "generate a marketing strategy for a new mobile app" will result in a strategy that focuses on promoting and reaching the target audience for the app.

Another advantage of using ChatGPT for business plan and marketing strategy generation is its ability to generate a wide variety of plans and strategies. Since it has been trained on a large amount of text data, it has a deep understanding of different types of businesses, marketing techniques and language and tone used in writing business and marketing plans. This means that it can generate plans and strategies that will appeal to a wide range of audiences and situations.

One popular use case for ChatGPT in generating business plans and marketing strategies is for entrepreneurs and small business owners. ChatGPT can be used to generate business plans and marketing strategies, providing a helpful tool for generating ideas, structuring arguments, and organizing information. This can save a lot of time for entrepreneurs and small business owners and also open up new possibilities for creative expression.

Another use case for ChatGPT in generating business plans and marketing strategies is for large companies and organizations. ChatGPT can be used to generate plans and strategies for new products, services or marketing campaigns. This can provide a valuable tool for generating ideas, identifying target audiences and developing effective strategies for reaching them. Additionally, ChatGPT can be used to generate plans and strategies for different departments, such as marketing, sales, and operations, providing a comprehensive approach to business planning and strategy development.

Example Prompts and Output

Prompt: "Generate a business plan for a new e-commerce startup"
Output: "Our e-commerce startup aims to provide customers with a wide variety of high-quality products at competitive prices. Our strategy includes building a strong online presence through SEO and social media marketing, implementing a user-friendly and visually appealing website design, and offering fast and reliable shipping options.
Additionally, we plan to differentiate ourselves by providing excellent customer service and

offering a loyalty program to encourage repeat business. We anticipate significant growth in the first year, with projected revenue of $5 million.

Prompt: "Generate a marketing strategy for a new mobile app"
Output: "Our mobile app aims to connect users with local events and activities in their area. Our target audience is 18-35-year-olds who are looking for new things to do. Our marketing strategy includes a strong social media campaign targeting this age group, influencer partnerships, and a referral program to incentivize current users to bring in new users. Additionally, we will be working with local businesses to offer exclusive deals and discounts to our app users. Our goal is to reach 100,000 active users within the first six months and continue to grow from there.

17. Generating news articles and reports

One of the key advantages of using ChatGPT for news article and report generation is its ability to understand the context and intent behind a prompt. This allows it to generate articles and reports that are relevant and appropriate for a given topic. For example, a prompt such as "generate a news article on the latest developments in the field of renewable energy" will result in an article that covers the latest research and innovations in the field, while a prompt such as "generate a report on the economic impact of the COVID-19 pandemic" will result in a report that provides a detailed analysis of the economic effects of the pandemic.

Another advantage of using ChatGPT for news article and report generation is its ability to generate a wide variety of articles and reports. Since it has been trained on a large amount of text data, it has a deep understanding of different news styles and formats, and the language and tone used in writing news articles and reports. This means that it can generate articles and reports that will appeal to a wide range of audiences and situations.

One popular use case for ChatGPT in generating news articles and reports is in the field of journalism. ChatGPT can be used by journalists and news organizations to generate articles and reports, providing a helpful tool for generating ideas, structuring arguments, and organizing information. This can save a lot of time for journalists and news organizations and also open up new possibilities for creative expression.

Another use case for ChatGPT in generating news articles and reports is in the field of business and finance. ChatGPT can be used by companies and organizations to generate reports on market trends, industry analysis, and financial performance, providing a helpful tool for generating ideas, structuring arguments, and organizing information.

Example Prompts and Output

Prompt: "Generate a news article on the latest developments in the field of renewable energy"
Output: "The field of renewable energy has seen significant advancements in recent years, with a particular focus on solar and wind power. A new breakthrough in solar cell technology has resulted in panels that are more efficient and cost-effective than ever before. Additionally, wind turbine designs have been optimized to generate more power with fewer materials. These developments have the potential to greatly increase the feasibility and sustainability of renewable energy sources.

Prompt: "Generate a report on the economic impact of the COVID-19 pandemic"
Output: "The COVID-19 pandemic has had a significant impact on the global economy, resulting in widespread job loss and economic downturn. Industries such as tourism, retail, and hospitality have been hit particularly hard. However, some industries such as technology and e-commerce have seen an increase in demand. This report will provide a detailed

analysis of the economic effects of the pandemic on various industries, as well as the measures being taken by governments and organizations to mitigate the damage and support economic recovery. Additionally, this report will also explore potential long-term effects of the pandemic on the global economy and potential opportunities for growth in the post-pandemic era. Overall, the COVID-19 pandemic has highlighted the need for greater economic resilience and diversification to better weather future crises.

18. Generating resumes and cover letters

One of the key advantages of using ChatGPT for resume and cover letter generation is its ability to understand the context and intent behind a prompt. This allows it to generate resumes and cover letters that are relevant and appropriate for a given job or industry. For example, a prompt such as "generate a resume for a software engineer position" will result in a resume that highlights the skills and experience relevant to a software engineering role, while a prompt such as "generate a cover letter for a marketing internship" will result in a letter that emphasizes the qualifications and enthusiasm of the candidate for the marketing industry.

Another advantage of using ChatGPT for resume and cover letter generation is its ability to generate a wide variety of resumes and cover letters. Since it has been trained on a large amount of text data, it has a deep understanding of different industries, job requirements and language and tone used in writing resumes and cover letters. This means that it can generate resumes and cover letters that will appeal to a wide range of audiences and situations.

One popular use case for ChatGPT in generating resumes and cover letters is for job seekers. ChatGPT can be used to generate resumes and cover letters, providing a helpful tool for generating ideas, structuring arguments, and organizing information. This can save a lot of time for job seekers and also open up new possibilities for creative expression.

Another use case for ChatGPT in generating resumes and cover letters is for human resources professionals. ChatGPT can be used to generate resumes and cover letters for various job positions, providing a helpful tool for identifying the best candidates and structuring the recruitment process.

While ChatGPT is an incredibly powerful tool for resume and cover letter generation, it is important to note that it is not perfect. Like any AI model, it is only as good as the data it has been trained on. This means that it may generate resumes and cover letters that are inaccurate, unrealistic, or otherwise inappropriate. Therefore, it is important to always review the output of ChatGPT and make sure that it aligns with your values and goals, and also to cross-check with human review.

Example Prompts and Output

Prompt: "Generate a resume for a software engineer position"
Output: "I am a highly skilled software engineer with experience in developing and maintaining complex software systems. I have a strong background in programming languages such as Python, Java and C++. I am also well-versed in Agile development methodologies and have experience working in both Linux and Windows environments. I am a quick learner and am able to adapt to new technologies and programming languages quickly. I am excited about the opportunity to contribute my skills and experience to your organization.

Prompt: "Generate a cover letter for a marketing internship"

Output: "I am writing to express my interest in the marketing internship with your company. I am currently pursuing a degree in marketing and have completed coursework in market research, advertising, and branding. I am eager to apply my knowledge and skills to a real-world setting and am excited about the opportunity to learn from the experienced professionals at your organization. I am a hardworking, dedicated individual with strong communication and analytical skills. I am confident that my skills and experience would be an asset to your team and I am eager to contribute to your marketing efforts. Additionally, I am highly motivated to learn about the latest trends and strategies in the industry and am excited about the opportunity to work with your company's cutting-edge marketing techniques. I would greatly appreciate the opportunity to discuss my qualifications and enthusiasm for this internship further. Thank you for considering my application.

19. Generating product or service descriptions

One example of ChatGPT's use in product description writing is in the e-commerce industry. Online retailers can use the model to generate detailed and compelling descriptions for their products, resulting in increased sales and customer satisfaction. For example, an e-commerce website that sells clothing could use ChatGPT to write descriptions for their products, such as "This sleek and stylish jacket is made from a high-quality material that will keep you warm on the coldest of days. The modern design features a zip-up front and multiple pockets, making it the perfect addition to your wardrobe."

Another example of ChatGPT's use is in the service industry. Businesses can use the model to write descriptions of their services, making it easier for potential customers to understand what they offer. For example, a consulting firm could use ChatGPT to write a description of their services, such as "Our consulting firm specializes in helping businesses increase their efficiency and profitability. We offer a wide range of services, including market research, financial analysis, and strategic planning. Our team of experts will work with you to identify and implement the best solutions for your business."

By using ChatGPT, businesses can generate high-quality, compelling product descriptions that can help to increase sales and customer satisfaction.

Example Prompts and Output

Prompt: "Write a product description for a new brand of organic shampoo"
Output:
"Introducing our new line of organic shampoo, made with only the finest natural ingredients. Formulated with nourishing ingredients like argan oil and aloe vera, our shampoo will leave your hair feeling soft and healthy. Our unique blend of essential oils will give your hair a refreshing scent, while also promoting hair growth. Free from harsh chemicals and synthetic fragrances, our shampoo is safe for all hair types. Give your hair the natural care it deserves with our new organic shampoo."

Prompt: "Write a service description for a home cleaning company"
Output:
"Looking for a reliable and thorough home cleaning service? Look no further than our company! Our team of expert cleaners will leave your home spotless, taking care of everything from dusting and vacuuming to scrubbing bathrooms and kitchens. We use only the highest-quality cleaning products, ensuring a deep clean every time. Our flexible scheduling options and competitive rates make it easy to fit a cleaning into your busy schedule. Give yourself the gift of a clean home and book a cleaning with us today!"

Prompt: "Write a product description for a new type of smartwatch"
Output:
"Introducing our new smartwatch, designed with the latest technology to make your life easier. With features like fitness tracking, sleep monitoring, and phone notifications, this watch will be your new go-to accessory. The watch face is customizable with a variety of watch faces and widgets, so you can make it your own. It also comes with built-in GPS and a heart rate monitor. The battery life is long-lasting and it is compatible with both iOS and Android devices. Upgrade your daily routine with our new smartwatch."

As we can see from these examples, ChatGPT can take a prompt and generate a human-like product or service description that is informative and engaging. The generated descriptions are detailed, with a good structure, and also providing all the necessary information about the product or service.

20. Generating creative and compelling ad copy

One example of ChatGPT's use in ad copy generation is in the marketing industry. Businesses can use the model to generate ad copy that is both creative and persuasive, which can help to increase the effectiveness of their advertising campaigns. For example, a company that sells a new type of energy drink could use ChatGPT to generate ad copy such as "Tired of feeling sluggish and drained? Try our new energy drink! Made with natural ingredients, it'll give you the boost you need to tackle your day. With a great taste, you'll forget you're even drinking an energy drink. Try it now and feel the difference!"

Another example of ChatGPT's use is in the advertising industry. Advertisers can use the model to generate ad copy that is both catchy and effective in catching the audience attention. For example, a company that sells a new type of car could use ChatGPT to generate ad copy such as "Experience the thrill of the open road with our new car. With sleek lines, advanced technology and a powerful engine, it's guaranteed to turn heads. Plus, with a spacious interior and comfortable seating, you'll never want to leave the driver's seat. Test drive it today and experience the difference!"

In addition to being used in ad copy generation, ChatGPT can be used in a variety of other applications such as content generation, language translation, and customer service. ChatGPT's ability to generate human-like text makes it a versatile tool that can be used in a wide range of industries.

With ChatGPT, businesses can create ad copy that is both creative and persuasive, which can help to increase sales and customer engagement.

Example Prompts and Output

Prompt: "Generate ad copy for a new type of toothpaste"
Output:
"Say goodbye to sensitive teeth and hello to a brighter, healthier smile with our new toothpaste. Formulated with a unique blend of natural ingredients, it gently and effectively whitens teeth while also strengthening enamel and reducing sensitivity. Plus, the refreshing mint flavor will leave your mouth feeling clean and fresh. Upgrade your oral care routine and try our toothpaste today."

Prompt: "Generate ad copy for a new type of mattress"
Output:
"Sick of tossing and turning at night? Our new mattress is here to help. Made with the latest technology and materials, it provides the perfect balance of support and comfort, so you can sleep soundly through the night. Plus, it's designed to reduce motion transfer, so you won't be disturbed by your partner's movements. Say goodbye to restless nights and hello to restful sleep with our new mattress."

Prompt: "Generate ad copy for a new type of running shoe"
Output:
"Experience the ultimate in comfort and performance with our new running shoe. Designed with the latest technology, it provides superior support and cushioning, so you can run longer and stronger. The breathable upper keeps your feet cool and dry, while the durable outsole provides excellent traction. Whether you're training for a marathon or just running for fun, our shoe will help you reach your goals. Try them today and feel the difference."

As we can see from these examples, ChatGPT can take a prompt and generate ad copy that is creative, compelling and persuasive. The ad copy is catchy, it highlights the benefits of the product and it's easy to understand. ChatGPT can also generate ad copy that is relevant to the target audience and it is able to use appropriate language, tone and style. This makes it a powerful tool for businesses and advertisers looking to create effective ad campaigns.

How Can Companies Improve Customer Service with ChatGPT?

With ChatGPT's advanced capabilities, businesses can now create bots that can respond to user queries quickly, accurately, and professionally - making it a great solution for any business looking to streamline their customer service operations while improving their relationship with those they serve.

There are multiple ways in which ChatGPT can benefit customer service. It allows businesses to create automated responses to user inquiries in real time. This drastically reduces wait times for customers, increases customer satisfaction, and allows companies to tailor their messages more accurately according to individual contexts.

Additionally, the emotion recognition technology built into ChatGPT's platform can help users better understand how customers feel about their product or service offerings which can be used to further customize the conversation and ensure that each user feels heard. Secondly, ChatGPT enables businesses to measure sentiment during conversations which helps them identify topics related to specific queries; this ensures companies craft messages tailored specifically for their target demographics.

Furthermore, by leveraging deep learning algorithms during conversations ChatGPT-enabled bots are able to recognize requests quickly and respond accordingly; this makes it easier for businesses of all sizes leverage this technology without needing extensive technical support teams on hand at all times.

The powerful integration capabilities of ChatGPT make it easy for companies to sync existing business systems such as CRM software or accounting solutions with it; this eliminates manual data entry requirements by agents using traditional customer service platforms and frees up resources so they can focus on tasks that would see better returns when handled manually rather than automated processes through AI technology such as chatbots.

The key to success in customer service is to use ChatGPT to efficiently and effectively handle customer service issues that can be automated, freeing up valuable time for personnel to provide the human touch where it is a higher priority.

Large Companies Using ChatGPT to Improve Customer Service

There are a number of large companies currently utilizing ChatGPT to improve their customer service operations. Some top examples include Microsoft, Hyundai, Avis Budget Group, JetBlue, eBay, and PepsiCo. Each of these companies has seen significant success in using ChatGPT to provide critical customer support services quickly and accurately.

Microsoft, for example, uses the technology to provide real-time sentiment analysis during conversations with customers which helps them better understand how customers feel about their products and services. Additionally, both Avis Budget Group and JetBlue have successfully implemented ChatGPT bots that can recite flight updates in real time as well as answer frequently asked questions from customers directly.

Meanwhile, eBay has used the technology to simplify the buyer journey by utilizing bots to fill out order forms and facilitate quick question/answer sessions between buyers and sellers.

Lastly, PepsiCo has leveraged its AI-powered chatbot solutions to reduce wait times while providing personalized recommendations based on customer preferences. All of these companies serve as great examples of how businesses can utilize this powerful AI platform in order to revolutionize their customer service experience!

How Small Business can use ChatGPT to Enhance Customer Service

Smaller businesses can also reap the benefits of using ChatGPT to improve customer service. For example, companies with limited resources can use its natural language processing (NLP) capabilities to automate responses to commonly-asked customer inquiries in real time. This eliminates the need for lengthy manual input from agents and allows them to focus on other key tasks.

Many small businesses use business sytems which they can connect (e.g., CRM software or accounting platforms) with the AI platform seamlessly so that customer data entry is automated and any necessary adjustments are handled quickly and easily.

By taking advantage of these features, small businesses can ensure they're providing every customer with an optimized experience while cutting back on unnecessary costs associated with traditional customer service operations.

How Can Marketing Departments Use ChatGPT?

Marketing departments can leverage the power of ChatGPT to create a more personalized experience for their customers. It can be used to create personalized messages tailored to individual customers' needs, allowing them to build greater loyalty and trust among customers.

Additionally, its sentiment analysis features can provide insights into customer sentiment and feedback, allowing marketing teams to better understand their target market and adjust strategies accordingly.

Moreover, companies can utilize ChatGPT's integration capabilities to connect their marketing platforms (e.g., email software or social media channels) and gain access to valuable customer data – such as purchase activity and website interactions – in order to optimize campaigns and maximize ROI.

By using this AI-powered technology effectively, marketing departments are able to effectively tailor their strategies while also reducing costs associated with traditional methods of communication.

Companies that are Using ChatGPT in their Marketing Efforts

There are numerous marketing teams who are using ChatGPT to improve their strategies and maximize ROI. For example, Adidas is using ChatGPT to create personalized messages for its customers as part of its overall customer engagement strategy. By leveraging the platform's natural language processing capabilities and sentiment analysis tools, they can customize each message based on individual preferences and provide customers with a more personalized experience.

Additionally, Honda is leveraging the platform's integration capabilities to connect its existing business systems (e.g., CRM software or accounting platforms) with the AI technology in order to gain access to valuable customer data such as purchase activity or website interactions. This allows them to optimize campaigns while cutting back on costs associated with traditional methods of communication.

These are just two examples of how marketing departments are utilizing ChatGPT technology; there are certainly many more companies out there leveraging this powerful AI-based technology effectively.

What Do Marketing Leaders Say about ChatGPT?

Famous marketing experts have been singing the praises of ChatGPT, pointing to its ability to create a more personalized customer experience and its integration capabilities as major benefits for companies.

For example, industry leader Seth Godin has said that ChatGPT's ability to provide personalized messages tailored to individual customers' needs "will make all the difference in creating loyal and engaged users."

Similarly, marketer Mark Cuban has praised ChatGPT for its potential to maximize ROI by helping companies access valuable customer data and optimize their campaigns accordingly. As these examples show, there is no shortage of enthusiasm from marketing experts about the potential of ChatGPT for increasing customer engagement and improving ROI.

Marketing Agencies and ChatGPT

A number of prominent marketing agencies have begun leveraging ChatGPT technology to improve customer service, maximize customer engagement, and increase operational efficiency.

Here are some examples of how they're using it:

- Digitas is leveraging ChatGPT for automated customer segmentation and targeted content recommendations.
- Dentsu Aegis Network is utilizing ChatGPT for customer service interactions via virtual assistants, allowing customers to get answers in real-time.
- Wunderman Thompson is leveraging ChatGPT capabilities for personalized email campaigns and website experiences.
- Ogilvy & Mather is also utilizing ChatGPT for customer service purposes such as automated ticket filing and chatbot-based FAQs.

Overall, these are just a few examples of how prominent marketing agencies are now utilizing the power of ChatGPT technology in their operations — allowing them to save time and money while improving the experience they provide for their customers.

Example Prompts and Output

Prompt: "What are the key features of a successful social media campaign?"
Output: "A successful social media campaign should have a clear target audience, a compelling message, a consistent brand voice, a strong call-to-action, and the ability to track and analyze metrics for ongoing optimization. It should also be able to engage with their audience through comments, messages, stories, and utilize visual and video content. It's also important to use the right social media platform that aligns with the audience and the campaign objective."

Prompt: "What are the advantages of influencer marketing?"
Output: "Influencer marketing can help to increase brand awareness and credibility, drive website traffic and sales, and reach a targeted audience. Influencers have a loyal following and can help to generate buzz and positive word-of-mouth for a brand. They also have the ability to create authentic and engaging content that resonates with their followers.

Prompt: "What are the best practices for email marketing campaigns?"

Output: "Best practices for email marketing campaigns include segmenting your email list, personalizing your subject line and message, using a clear and compelling call-to-action, optimizing for mobile, regularly testing and optimizing your email campaigns, and adhering to laws such as CAN-SPAM Act."

Prompt: "How can we measure the ROI of our PPC campaign?"
Output: "To measure the ROI of a PPC campaign, you can track key metrics such as click-through rate (CTR), conversion rate, cost per acquisition (CPA), and return on ad spend (ROAS). You can also use tools such as Google Analytics to track website traffic and conversions from your PPC ads. It's also important to regularly review and optimize your campaigns based on this data, to ensure that you are getting the best return on investment."

ChatGPT in Education

Here are four ways that ChatGPT is being used in education:

1. ChatGPT can be used to teach students complex concepts in a more engaging and interactive way by providing real-time dialogue and feedback. In addition, it is able to simulate conversations that could take place in a physical classroom environment, allowing teachers to discuss topics such as bullying and stress management without putting any student at risk of embarrassment or shame.
2. By leveraging its personalization capabilities, ChatGPT can provide customized learning experiences tailored to the individual needs of each student. For example, it can provide personalized feedback for each learner based on their performance, helping increase motivation and engagement. It can also generate insights about the progress of each student and help teachers identify areas of improvement, allowing them to make more informed decisions about lesson planning and curriculum development.
3. ChatGPT can also be used as an effective collaboration tool in

educational settings, helping multiple students engage with each other on projects or course material in an efficient manner. Its ability to handle natural language processing tasks makes it well suited for tasks such as fact-checking or comprehension checks that would otherwise require extensive manual labor from teachers or teaching assistants.
4. Finally, ChatGPT's integration capabilities allow it to be easily integrated into existing educational platforms, making the transition to AI-powered learning smoother for educators and learners alike.

With its wide range of features and potential applications, ChatGPT can become an essential tool for modern education systems all around the world.

Examples of ChatGPT in Higher Education

Higher education institutions are increasingly leveraging ChatGPT to provide improved services for both students and staff.

Here are some examples of how higher education institutions are using ChatGPT today:

- Stanford University is utilizing ChatGPT in their admissions process, creating an AI chatbot which automatically reviews applications for completeness and accuracy.
- The University of Edinburgh is using ChatGPT to power their virtual assistant — a 24-hour customer service bot which helps answer questions and provides information about the university's offerings.
- Harvard Law School has implemented a ChatGPT-powered automated essay grading system, allowing them to quickly and accurately grade essays without having to manually read through each one.
- Oxford University is also leveraging ChatGPT capabilities in their course registration process, providing students with an AI-driven chatbot which can help them determine which courses best fit their needs.

Overall, these are just a few examples of how higher education institutions are utilizing the power of ChatGPT technology in order to improve the experience for both students and staff. By automating mundane tasks such as document analysis or customer service queries, universities are free to focus on more important aspects such as curriculum development or student engagement.

Example Prompts and Output

Prompt: "What is the main argument in Jane Austen's 'Pride and Prejudice'?"
Output: "The main argument in Jane Austen's 'Pride and Prejudice' is that societal pressure to marry for wealth and status often leads to misguided judgments and ultimately impedes the development of true love and understanding between individuals."

Prompt: "What is the significance of the color green in F. Scott Fitzgerald's 'The Great Gatsby'?"
Output: "In F. Scott Fitzgerald's 'The Great Gatsby', the color green symbolizes the longing for and the illusion of an unattainable American Dream, as well as the moral decay associated with the pursuit of wealth and status."

Prompt: "What is the role of the chorus in ancient Greek drama?"
Output: "The chorus in ancient Greek drama served several functions. They provided commentary on the action, represented the voice of the community, and provided a musical and rhythmic element to the performance."

Prompt: "What is the impact of the Industrial Revolution on society and literature?"
Output: "The Industrial Revolution had a significant impact on society and literature. It brought about economic, social, and technological changes that led to the emergence of a new urban working class and the displacement of traditional agricultural communities. This in turn led to a new sense of identity and a new set of literary themes and motifs in literature such as alienation, urbanization, and the dehumanizing effects of industrialization."

ChatGPT in Manufacturing

In recent years, the emergence of ChatGPT technology has revolutionized the manufacturing sector. It can be used in various areas of manufacturing, from controlling robotic production lines to analyzing data for quality control and optimization.

One of the most promising uses of ChatGPT in manufacturing is its ability to facilitate communication between machines and humans. Because ChatGPT can "speak" the same language as humans, it can be used to bridge the gap between people and robots — making factory operations smoother, more efficient, and more accurate.

For example, if a machine needs maintenance or repair work completed on it, ChatGPT could be used to send an alert message to the appropriate personnel, allowing them to quickly and easily address any issues that arise during production runs. ChatGPT can also be utilized for data extraction or analysis. By utilizing its NLP capabilities, ChatGPT can read through large amounts of unstructured data such as product specifications or engineering plans in a fraction of the time traditional methods would take. This enables manufacturers to quickly identify areas that may need improvement or require development — allowing them to stay ahead of the competition.

Finally, one area where ChatGPT is having a significant impact on manufacturing is automation. By using its deep learning algorithms, ChatGPT can detect patterns in large amounts of data — providing insights that can help automate certain processes such as order fulfillment or inventory management without requiring human intervention.

Automation has been an important factor in improving efficiency across many industries over the last few decades; however, with advances made by ChatGPT technology this process has been further streamlined for use in today's modern factories around the world. In conclusion, as an AI-powered natural language processing platform, ChatGPT is proving to be an invaluable asset for modern manufacturers across many industries all around the world.

With its ability to interpret text efficiently and think proactively about tasks at hand, it will continue to revolutionize how manufacturing businesses operate into the foreseeable future.

Companies Using ChatGPT in Manufacturing

A number of companies are now utilizing ChatGPT technology in their manufacturing processes to improve efficiency and reduce costs.

Here are some examples of how they're using it:
- ABB, a robotics and automation company, has implemented a conversational AI system powered by ChatGPT to automate manual inspection tasks such as visual inspection or measuring size and shape.
- Volkswagen is leveraging ChatGPT capabilities for their automated assembly line process, providing robots with natural language instructions on assembly tasks.
- Boeing uses ChatGPT in their supply chain management process, providing real-time information about the status of production and delivery via an AI chatbot.
- Siemens is also utilizing ChatGPT in the manufacturing process, creating an AI-driven virtual assistant which helps manage orders, analyze data from production lines and generate performance reports automatically.

Overall, these are just a few examples of how companies are utilizing the power of ChatGPT technology in their manufacturing processes — allowing them to save time and money while maintaining quality control.

Example Prompts and Output

Prompt: "What is the recommended torque for tightening this bolt?"
Output: "The recommended torque for tightening this bolt is X Newton-meters (Nm)."

Prompt: "What is the process for cleaning and maintaining this piece of equipment?"
Output: "The process for cleaning and maintaining this piece of equipment includes the following steps: 1) Turn off and unplug the equipment 2) Use a soft cloth and a mild detergent solution to wipe down all surfaces 3) Rinse the equipment with clean water 4) Dry the equipment thoroughly 5) Check for any signs of wear or damage 6) Lubricate any moving parts as necessary 7) Conduct a test run to ensure proper function."

Prompt: "What is the maximum operating temperature for this material?"
Output: "The maximum operating temperature for this material is X degrees Celsius (°C)."

Prompt: "What is the proper procedure for handling and storing this chemical?"
Output: "The proper procedure for handling and storing this chemical includes wearing personal protective equipment (PPE) such as gloves and goggles, storing the chemical in a cool, dry place away from heat sources and

incompatible materials, and following the proper labeling and disposal guidelines."

ChatGPT and Professional Speakers

Professional speakers can use ChatGPT to help them prepare for their speeches by generating speech outlines, key points, and even complete speech scripts. They can also use it to practice and refine their delivery by having the model generate responses to potential questions or objections that they may encounter during their presentations.

Additionally, ChatGPT can be used to generate marketing and promotional materials, such as email newsletters, social media posts, and website content, to help promote their speaking engagements.

Example Prompts and Output

Here are a few examples of prompts and corresponding output that a professional speaker might use with ChatGPT:

Prompt: "Outline for a motivational speech on overcoming adversity"

Output: Introduction:

- Share personal story of overcoming adversity

- Define adversity and its impact on individuals and society

Body:

- Discuss the importance of mindset in overcoming adversity
- Provide strategies for developing a positive mindset
- Share examples of successful individuals who have overcome adversity

Conclusion:

- Recap key points
- Encourage audience to take action and overcome their own adversities

Prompt: "Introduction for a keynote speech on the future of technology"

Output: "Good evening, everyone,
It's an honor to be here today to speak with you about the future of technology. As we stand on the cusp of a new era, one marked by rapid advancements in artificial intelligence, biotechnology, and the Internet of Things, it's never been more important to understand and stay ahead of the curve.

The next few years will see some incredible breakthroughs in how we live and work, and I am excited to share with you some of the most exciting possibilities on the horizon.

Are you ready to discover what the future holds?"

Prompt: "Key points for a speech on leadership"

Output:

- The importance of clear communication
- Empowering and trusting your team
- Leading by example
- Adapting to change
- Encouraging creativity and innovation
- Taking responsibility for your actions and decisions
- Continuously learning and improving
- Building a positive and inclusive culture
- These are just a few examples of how professional speakers might use ChatGPT to generate speech outlines, introductions, and key points. The output from ChatGPT can be used as a starting point, which can be further edited, refined and customized by the professional speaker.

ChatGPT and Business Coaches

Business coaches can use ChatGPT in a variety of ways to help them with their coaching practice. Here are a few examples:

- Generating coaching exercises and activities: Business coaches can use ChatGPT to generate prompts and questions for coaching exercises and activities that can be used to help clients identify and work through specific issues or challenges.

- Creating coaching materials: Business coaches can use ChatGPT to generate handouts, worksheets, and other materials that they can use in their coaching sessions.

- Developing coaching plans: Business coaches can use ChatGPT to generate customized coaching plans for individual clients based on their specific needs and goals.

- Writing content: Business coaches can use ChatGPT to generate blog posts, articles, e-books and other content that can be used to promote their coaching practice and establish themselves as thought leaders in their field.

- Responding to client's inquiry: Coaches can use ChatGPT to quickly respond to their client's inquiries, answering questions and providing guidance, without having to spend a lot of time on crafting each response.

- Generating testimonials: Coaches can use ChatGPT to generate testimonials from satisfied clients that can be used to promote their coaching practice.

It's important to note that the output generated by ChatGPT should be used as a starting point and then tailored to the specific client, as well as reviewed and approved by the coach before it is shared with the client.

Example Prompts and Output

Here are a few examples of prompts and corresponding output that a business coach might use with ChatGPT:

Prompt: "Coaching exercises for improving time management"

Output:

- "Time Audit: Have the client track their time for a week, noting how they spend their time each day. Review the results with the client and identify areas where they can make adjustments to be more efficient.

- "Prioritization Matrix: Have the client create a matrix of tasks, ranking them based on importance and urgency. This will help them focus on the most important tasks and avoid getting bogged down in less important ones.

- "Schedule Review: Review the client's schedule with them and identify any recurring meetings or tasks that can be consolidated or eliminated.

- "Eliminate Distractions: Have the client identify the top distractions that disrupt their workflow and develop a plan to eliminate or minimize them."

Prompt: "Coaching plan for a new business owner"

Output:

Introduction:

- Establish goals and objectives for the coaching engagement
- Define and review the coaching process

Assessment:

- Review the client's current business situation and identify areas of strength and opportunity
- Identify any challenges or obstacles that the client is facing

Action Plan:

- Develop a customized action plan to address the identified challenges and opportunities
- Establish milestones and track progress
- Provide support and guidance as the client implements the plan

Review and Adjust:

- Review progress and adjust the plan as needed
- Celebrate successes and address any roadblocks
- Prepare the client for ongoing success"

Prompt: "Tips for conducting a successful performance review"

Output:

- Set clear, measurable goals and expectations with the employee before the review
- Be specific and provide examples when giving feedback, both positive and constructive
- Encourage open communication and actively listen to the employee's perspective
- Share the employee's strengths and areas for growth
- Develop a plan for improvement and set follow-up goals
- Provide continuous support and coaching to help the employee reach their potential

These are just a few examples of how business coaches might use ChatGPT to generate coaching exercises, plans, and tips. The output from ChatGPT can be used as a starting point, which can be further edited, refined, and customized by the coach to fit the specific client's needs.

Chat GPT and Sales Managers

Sales managers can use ChatGPT in a variety of ways to help them with their sales management responsibilities. Here are a few examples:

1. Generating sales scripts: Sales managers can use ChatGPT to generate scripts for their sales team to use when communicating with potential customers. The scripts can be tailored to different types of customers and products, and can be used to effectively communicate the key benefits of the product or service.
2. Creating sales reports: Sales managers can use ChatGPT to generate detailed sales reports that can be used to track performance, identify trends, and make informed decisions.
3. Developing sales strategies: Sales managers can use ChatGPT to generate customized sales strategies for different products, markets, and customer segments.
4. Responding to customer inquiries: Sales managers can use ChatGPT to quickly respond to customer inquiries, answering questions, and providing information about products and

services, without having to spend a lot of time crafting each response.
5. Generating sales emails: Sales managers can use ChatGPT to generate effective sales emails that can be used to generate leads and close deals.
6. Creating sales training materials: Sales managers can use ChatGPT to generate training materials, such as presentations, handouts, and quizzes, to train their sales team on new products, sales techniques, and best practices.

It's important to note that the output generated by ChatGPT should be reviewed and approved by the sales manager before it is shared with the sales team or customers.

Example Prompts and Output

Here are a few examples of prompts and corresponding output that a sales manager might use with ChatGPT:

Prompt: "Script for a sales pitch for a new CRM software"
Output:
"Hello,
I'm reaching out to introduce you to our new CRM software. This software is designed to help businesses like yours streamline their sales process and increase productivity.

Our CRM software allows you to manage your customer data in one centralized location, track sales progress, and generate reports. It also includes features like automated email and text message follow-ups, appointment scheduling, and lead tracking.
I'd like to schedule a quick call with you to discuss how our CRM software can benefit your business and answer any questions you may have. Would that be something you'd be interested in?"

Prompt: "Sales report for the last quarter"
Output:
"Sales Report for Q3 2021:

Total revenue for the quarter was $5,000,000
Total number of deals closed: 200
Average deal size: $25,000
Top-performing salesperson: John Smith (closed 25 deals)
Top-performing product: Product A (generated $1,000,000 in revenue)
Weakest-performing product: Product B (generated $250,000 in revenue)
Top-performing market: North America (generated $2,500,000 in revenue)
Opportunities for improvement: Low close rate on deals over $50,000 and lack of leads generated in the Asia market.
Prompt: "Email template for following up with a potential customer"

Output:
"Subject: Following up on our conversation

Hello [Name],

I hope this email finds you well. I wanted to follow up on the conversation we had about [product/service]. I understand that you're currently in the research phase and trying to determine which solution would be the best fit for your business.
I wanted to remind you of the key benefits of our [product/service], such as [benefit 1], [benefit 2], and [benefit 3]. I would like to schedule a call to discuss this further and answer any questions you may have.
Please let me know what your availability is like next week and we'll work out a time that works for you.

Best regards,
[Your name]"

These are just a few examples of how sales managers might use ChatGPT to generate sales scripts, reports, and templates. The output from ChatGPT can be used as a starting point, which can be further edited, refined, and customized by the sales manager to fit the specific needs of the sales team and customers.

ChatGPT and the Legal Profession

ChatGPT technology has had a major impact on the legal profession. ChatGPT can help provide lawyers with a wide range of benefits — ranging from improved document analysis to better client satisfaction levels.

One of the primary uses of ChatGPT in the legal profession is document analysis. By leveraging its ability to understand written text, ChatGPT can be used to quickly and accurately identify key words or phrases from large sets of documents. This allows lawyers to find relevant information quickly and easily — something that would have taken hours or even days for humans to accomplish manually.

In addition, it can also be used to compare different contracts or documents for similarities or differences in language or phrasing — ensuring accuracy when it comes time to present evidence in court.

Another way ChatGPT is being used by the legal profession is through automated case tracking systems. By using its deep learning algorithms, ChatGPT can monitor cases as they move through various stages — providing lawyers with timely updates on their progress so they can focus their attention on tasks that require more manual intervention.

In addition, these systems are able to track multiple cases at once, allowing lawyers to stay up-to-date on all proceedings without having to jump between multiple sources at all times.

Finally, ChatGPT's natural language processing capabilities are being utilized as a customer service tool in many law firms as well. By providing clients with an AI-powered chatbot that understands their questions and concerns and responds appropriately via text message or email, it helps reduce wait times and improve customer satisfaction levels overall — something that is becoming increasingly important in today's global marketplace.

In conclusion, ChatGPT technology has had a significant impact on the legal profession over the last few years — helping ease workloads, speed up processes and improve overall customer satisfaction levels for law firms around the world. With advances in this area continuing at a rapid pace and more applications being developed every day, it stands ready to revolutionize how law firms do business into the foreseeable future.

Law Firms Using ChatGPT

There are a number of law firms that are already utilizing ChatGPT technology to improve their operational processes and customer service capabilities.

Here are a few examples:

- Clifford Chance, one of the world's largest international law firms, is using ChatGPT to power an AI-driven smart assistant which allows users to search their extensive knowledge base quickly and easily.
- Covington & Burling LLP is utilizing ChatGPT to automate document analysis and legal research tasks, saving considerable time in their everyday workflow.
- White & Case is leveraging ChatGPT's natural language processing capabilities to provide clients with an AI-powered virtual assistant which can answer common queries or direct them to further resources accordingly.
- Latham & Watkins is utilizing ChatGPT to provide automated case tracking systems, letting lawyers quickly and accurately determine where cases are in the process at any given time.

Overall, these law firms are just a few examples of how ChatGPT technology is being used by legal professionals around the world — helping them streamline their daily operations and generate better results for their clients.

Example Prompts and Output

Prompt: "What is the statute of limitations for filing a personal injury lawsuit in state X?"
Output: "In state X, the statute of limitations for filing a personal injury lawsuit is X years from the date of the incident."

Prompt: "What are the elements of a breach of contract claim?"
Output: "The elements of a breach of contract claim typically include: (1) the existence of a valid contract, (2) performance by one party, (3) breach of contract by the other party, (4) causation and (5) damages."

Prompt: "What is the standard of proof in a criminal case?"
Output: "In a criminal case, the prosecution must prove the defendant's guilt "beyond a reasonable doubt."

Prompt: "What is the difference between a civil and a criminal case?"
Output: "A civil case involves a dispute between two or more parties in which one party sues the other for a legal remedy such as

money damages. Criminal cases, on the other hand, involve an action that is considered to be against the state or society as a whole and is punishable by fines, imprisonment, or both."

ChatGPT and Healthcare

ChatGPT technology has become increasingly popular in the medical profession as a method for accelerating time-consuming and mundane tasks. By utilizing AI technologies such as natural language processing and machine learning, medical professionals are able to dramatically reduce their workload while ensuring accuracy and consistency in their work.

Here are some examples of how ChatGTP is benefiting the medical profession:
- Surgical teams are using ChatGPT Virtual Assistants to quickly review patient information during pre and post-op procedures, allowing surgeons to focus more on the task at hand.
- Diagnostic teams can utilize ChatGPT capabilities to analyze laboratory results more accurately and efficiently — saving significant time in the process.
- Hospitals are utilizing ChatGPT-powered chatbots to manage administrative tasks such as appointment scheduling or filling out forms.
- Clinical researchers are able to leverage ChatGPT capabilities for faster data collection, enabling them to perform

large scale studies with greater ease and precision.

Overall, these are just a few examples of how ChatGTP technology is benefiting the medical profession by allowing medical professionals to do their jobs faster while ensuring accuracy and consistency in their work. By freeing up valuable time and resources, healthcare providers are able to provide improved services for patients while reducing costs associated with long hours or extensive paperwork processes.

Example Prompts and Output

Prompt: "What is the recommended dosage for amoxicillin in children?"
Output: "The recommended dosage for amoxicillin in children is 25-45 mg/kg/day in divided doses every 8-12 hours. The maximum daily dose should not exceed 90 mg/kg."

Prompt: "What are the contraindications for the use of metformin?"
Output: "Contraindications for the use of metformin include renal impairment, known hypersensitivity to the drug, and conditions such as metabolic acidosis or severe infection."

Prompt: "What is the treatment for stage 2 hypertension?"

Output: "Treatment for stage 2 hypertension typically includes lifestyle changes such as weight loss, exercise, and a healthy diet. Medications such as thiazide diuretics, ACE inhibitors, and calcium channel blockers may also be prescribed to help lower blood pressure."

Prompt: "What is the interpretation of a positive ANA test?"
Output: "A positive ANA test indicates the presence of antinuclear antibodies in the blood. This can be seen in a variety of autoimmune disorders such as lupus, rheumatoid arthritis, and Sjogren's syndrome, but a positive ANA test alone is not diagnostic and further testing is needed to confirm a specific diagnosis."

Hospitals Using ChatGPT

A number of prominent hospitals are now utilizing ChatGPT technology to improve their operations and patient care.

Here are some examples of how they're using it:

- The Mayo Clinic has implemented a virtual assistant powered by ChatGPT that answers various medical questions and provides relevant information to patients seeking advice.

- Stanford Hospital is leveraging ChatGPT capabilities to automate healthcare workflow tasks such as transferring files or managing patient records.
- Kaiser Permanente is leveraging ChatGPT capabilities for their automated appointment scheduling system, allowing patients to book appointments quickly and conveniently through an AI chatbot.
- Johns Hopkins Hospital is also utilizing ChatGPT in the form of a virtual assistant to help monitor vital signs, enabling nurses to focus more on patient care rather than paperwork.

These are just a few examples of how prominent hospitals are now utilizing the power of ChatGPT technology in their operations — allowing them to save time and money while improving the care they provide for their patients.

Example Prompts and Output

Prompt: "What are the symptoms of a heart attack?" Output: "Symptoms of a heart attack can include chest pain or discomfort, upper body pain or discomfort in the arms, back, neck, jaw, or stomach, shortness of breath, breaking out in a cold sweat, and nausea."

Prompt: "How should a patient with a broken bone be treated?" Output: "A patient with a broken bone should be treated by immobilizing the affected limb to prevent further injury, administering pain medication, and seeking medical attention as soon as possible to have the bone properly set and casted."

Prompt: "What are the side effects of the medication Metformin?" Output: "Common side effects of Metformin include stomach upset, diarrhea, and nausea. Less common side effects include headache, chest pain, and trouble breathing. If any of these side effects are severe or do not go away, a doctor should be consulted."

Prompt: "What is the standard treatment for a patient with stage 3 lung cancer?" Output: "The standard treatment for a patient with stage 3 lung cancer typically includes a combination of surgery, radiation therapy and chemotherapy. The specific treatment plan may vary depending on factors such as the patient's overall health and the specific type of lung cancer."

ChatGPT and the Financial Industry

ChatGPT technology has been increasingly embraced by the financial industry as a means to modernize services and accelerate operations. Financial institutions are able to automate mundane tasks while still providing accurate and personalized services for their customers.

Here are some examples of how ChatGPT is being used in the financial industry:
- Banks are utilizing virtual assistants powered by ChatGPT to provide customers with automated banking services such as checking balances or transferring funds.
- Investment firms are leveraging ChatGPT capabilities to provide real-time analysis of stocks and portfolios, allowing clients to make more informed decisions with greater ease.
- Insurance companies are using ChatGPT-powered chatbots to process claims faster while improving customer service interactions through automated messaging systems.
- Credit card companies are now utilizing ChatGPT technology for fraud detection, enabling them to quickly

detect suspicious transactions before they occur.

Overall, these are just a few examples of how ChatGPT is being utilized by the financial industry to speed up operations and improve service efficiency — ultimately leading to improved customer satisfaction and reduced costs associated with manual paperwork processes.

Companies in the Financial Sector Using ChatGPT

A number of prominent companies in the financial sector, such as banks, investment firms, insurance providers, and credit card companies, are now leveraging ChatGPT technology to modernize their operations.

Here are some examples of how they're using it:

- JPMorgan Chase is leveraging ChatGPT capabilities for automated customer service interactions via virtual assistants, allowing customers to get answers or assistance in real-time.
- Morgan Stanley is utilizing ChatGPT-powered chatbots to provide clients with personalized investment advice and market analysis.

- USAA is leveraging ChatGPT for fraud detection through automated risk assessment tools.
- American Express is also utilizing ChatGPT for customer service purposes such as automated account management and payments processing.

Overall, these are just a few examples of how prominent companies in the financial sector are now utilizing the power of ChatGPT technology in their operations — allowing them to save time and money while improving the experience they provide for their customers.

Example Prompts and Output

Prompt: "What is the current stock price for Apple?"
Output: "As of market close on [date], the stock price for Apple is [current price]."

Prompt: "What are the projected earnings for the upcoming quarter for IBM?"
Output: "Based on analyst reports, IBM is projected to have earnings of [projected earnings] for the upcoming quarter."

Prompt: "What is the current interest rate for a 30-year fixed mortgage?"

Output: "The current interest rate for a 30-year fixed mortgage is [current rate] percent."

Prompt: "What is the current market trend for crude oil?"
Output: "Crude oil prices have been [current trend] in recent months, with a current price of [current price]."

The Transportation Industry and ChatGPT

The transportation industry has seen a rapid adoption of ChatGPT technology, with major companies in the sector now utilizing it to improve customer service and operational efficiency. This chapter will explore the various ways in which ChatGPT is being used in the transportation industry, discussing how companies are leveraging the technology to enhance their services and improve customer experience.

One of the primary ways in which ChatGPT is being utilized by transportation companies is for automated customer service interactions. From airlines to ride-hailing apps, many companies are now using virtual agents to handle inquiries and provide prompt answers to customers in real-time.

For example, Lyft recently launched its own virtual assistant called Butler that can answer common questions about ride availability and pricing without having to involve human customer service agents.

Another way that transportation companies are leveraging ChatGPT technology is for automated payment processing. Companies such as Uber and Grab have implemented

ChatGPT-powered systems that allow customers to pay for rides automatically through their smartphones or other connected devices. This helps streamline the payment process and makes transactions faster and more convenient for both drivers and passengers alike.

Transportation companies are also utilizing ChatGPT capabilities for logistics optimization — providing automated route planning services that can determine efficient routes for drivers as well as assist with real-time traffic updates and navigation suggestions. This helps ensure that drivers reach their destinations quickly while helping customers save time (and potentially money) on their trips.

Overall, ChatGPT technology is revolutionizing the way businesses operate within the transportation industry — allowing them to provide better customer experiences while simultaneously reducing costs associated with labor and operations management. Companies that make use of these innovative tools will surely stand out from the competition — positioning themselves as leaders in this constantly evolving field.

Examples of Transportation Companies Using ChatGPT

A number of prominent transportation companies have begun leveraging ChatGPT technology to improve customer service, optimize operational efficiency and automation, and improve customer experience.

Here are some examples of how they're using it:

- Delta Airlines is using ChatGPT for automated payment processing, allowing customers to pay for flights directly through their smartphones or other connected devices.
- Tesla is utilizing ChatGPT for logistics optimization — providing automated route planning services that can determine efficient routes for drivers as well as assist with real-time traffic updates and navigation suggestions.
- Uber recently launched its own virtual assistant called Eatsbot which leverages ChatGPT capabilities to answer customer inquiries in real-time.
- Amtrak is also utilizing ChatGPT technology to automate check-in processes, allowing customers to check in quickly without having to wait in line or speak with a representative.

Overall, these are just a few examples of how prominent transportation companies are now using the power of ChatGPT technology in their operations — allowing them to save time and money while providing customers with more seamless experiences.

Example Prompts and Output

Prompt: "Generate a press release announcing a new route for a bus company"

Output:
"We're excited to announce a new route for our bus company, which will make it easier for our customers to get to and from their destinations. The new route will connect several key locations in the city, including the downtown area, the airport, and a major shopping district. The new route will also feature more frequent service and extended hours of operation, making it more convenient for our customers to travel. We're committed to providing our customers with safe and reliable transportation, and this new route is a step in that direction.

Prompt: "Generate a script for a TV commercial for a new ride-sharing service"
Output:
"Are you tired of dealing with the hassle and expense of owning a car? Try our new ride-sharing service! With our app, you can easily request a ride at any time and be picked up by one of our professional drivers. Our service is

safe, reliable, and affordable, and you'll never have to worry about parking, traffic, or navigating unfamiliar areas. Plus, with our carpooling feature, you can share the ride and the cost with other passengers. Try our new ride-sharing service today and experience the freedom and convenience of on-demand transportation.

Prompt: "Generate a customer service script for resolving a complaint about a delay in a flight"
Output:
"We apologize for the delay in your flight. We understand how frustrating this can be and we're committed to resolving this issue as soon as possible. The delay was due to a technical issue with the aircraft, but we're working to have it resolved as soon as possible. In the meantime, we're providing our passengers with updates on the flight status and we'll do our best to make the wait as comfortable as possible. We apologize for any inconvenience this delay may have caused and we appreciate your patience. If you have any further questions or concerns, please don't hesitate to contact our customer service team. We understand the importance of getting you to your destination on time and we'll do everything we can to minimize the delay and get you on your way as soon as possible.

ChatGPT and Government

The use of ChatGPT technology in the government sector has grown exponentially in recent years. ChatGPT is being used to automate a number of tasks, from data processing and analysis to customer service inquiries. In this chapter, we'll take an in-depth look at how exactly ChatGPT is being utilized by government organizations around the world.

First and foremost, governments are adopting ChatGPT for its ability to automate manual processes. The technology can be used to quickly and accurately process data, allowing government agencies to save time and resources while improving accuracy. This automation also helps them focus on more important tasks like creating innovative policy solutions or responding to public feedback.

ChatGPT is also finding uses in customer service departments within government organizations. ChatGPT agents can understand what customers are asking and provide quick, accurate responses without needing human intervention. This saves valuable time and money for the organization while ensuring constituents get their questions answered promptly. More recently, government agencies have begun leveraging ChatGPT for decision-making capabilities—allowing them to make faster decisions with better accuracy than traditional methods.

From security surveillance to disaster management operations, ChatGPT can provide real-time insights that help governments identify trends faster and make more informed decisions based on accurate data analyses.

Governments are beginning to explore the use of ChatGPT for predictive analytics. This allows them to anticipate user requests before they even happen which allows for smoother interactions between citizens and their local governments.

Overall, it's clear that governments across the globe are beginning to leverage the power of ChatGTP technology — allowing them to save time and resources while providing citizens with higher quality services than ever before.

Examples of ChatGPT use by Government Agencies

In recent years, there have been a number of notable government agencies embracing the power of ChatGPT technology to improve operations and services.

Here are just a few examples:

- The United States Department of Defense is using ChatGPT for an automated security surveillance system which scans terrain and objects in order to detect potential threats.
- The United Kingdom's Government Digital Service is leveraging ChatGPT for predictive analytics to better anticipate users' needs before they even ask.
- The City of San Francisco has adopted ChatGPT for their 311 service which help citizens quickly access information or submit requests on a range of issues from public safety to infrastructure.
- The Australian government is utilizing ChatGPT capabilities to automate decision-making processes across multiple government departments, allowing them to make more informed decisions with greater accuracy and efficiency.

Overall, these are just a few examples of how governments around the world are using the power of ChatGPT technology — streamlining processes and improving customer experience while reducing costs.

Example Prompts and Output

Prompt: "Generate a press release announcing a new public transportation initiative"
Output:
"We're excited to announce a new public transportation initiative that will make it easier and more convenient for residents to get around our city. With the new initiative, we'll be expanding bus routes, increasing frequency of service, and introducing new technologies such as real-time bus tracking and mobile ticketing. The new initiative will also increase accessibility for people with disabilities, and make it easier for people to connect to other forms of transportation such as bike-sharing and ride-sharing services. This new initiative is part of our ongoing efforts to improve the quality of life for our residents and make our city more livable and sustainable.

Prompt: "Generate a script for a public service announcement on the importance of disaster preparedness"
Output:
"Are you prepared for a disaster? Natural disasters can happen at any time, and it's important to be ready. That's why we're reminding everyone to have a disaster plan in place. Make sure you have enough supplies to last for at least three days. Make a list of important phone numbers, and have a

designated meeting place for your family. Also, make sure you know the evacuation routes for your area. By being prepared, you can protect yourself and your loved ones in the event of a disaster. Remember, it's always better to be safe than sorry.

Prompt: "Generate a report on the economic impact of a new infrastructure project"
Output:
"The new infrastructure project is expected to have a significant economic impact on the region. The construction of the project is expected to generate thousands of jobs in the short-term and hundreds of jobs in the long-term. The project is also expected to attract new businesses and investment to the area, which will lead to further economic growth. Additionally, the improved infrastructure will make it easier for residents and businesses to access goods and services, which will boost productivity and efficiency. The total economic impact of the project is estimated to be in the billions of dollars over the next decade, which is a significant boost to the regional economy. The project is also expected to have a positive impact on the environment, by reducing traffic congestion and emissions, and providing improved access to alternative modes of transportation such as cycling and walking. The new infrastructure project will be a key driver of economic development in the region

and will help to create a more sustainable and livable community.

ChatGPT and Non-Profit Organizations

Non-profit organizations have embraced the power of ChatGPT technology to streamline their operations and maximize the impact of their work. This chapter will explore how exactly non-profits are leveraging ChatGPT and the potential benefits it can bring to their organizations.

One key use for ChatGPT in the non-profit sector is automating customer service inquiries. ChatGPT agents can understand what customers are asking and provide quick, accurate responses without needing human intervention. This saves valuable time and money while ensuring constituents get their questions answered promptly.

More recently, nonprofits are beginning to explore using ChatGPT for decision support purposes. By analyzing past data and activities, the technology can provide real-time insights that help non-profits identify trends faster and make more informed decisions when it comes to fundraising or promoting a cause.

Furthermore, organizations are utilizing ChatGPT to automate administrative tasks like scheduling appointments or managing volunteer databases which previously required significant manual labor. Automation helps free up staff members' time so they can focus on more important initiatives such as producing innovative programs or expanding outreach operations.

Overall, it's clear that ChatGPT is quickly becoming an invaluable asset for non-profit organizations around the world — enabling them to save resources while improving their overall operations and effectiveness.

Examples of Non-Profit Organizations Using ChatGPT

There are many non-profit organizations around the world leveraging ChatGPT technology to power various operations and services.

A few notable examples include:

- The American Red Cross is using ChatGPT for their blood donor appointment scheduling system, allowing donors to quickly find a donation center that fits their availability.
- WWF International is utilizing ChatGPT for their donations platform, providing users real-time insights into how their contributions are creating meaningful

- change for wildlife and nature conservation.
- UNICEF has implemented ChatGPT to monitor incoming data from different sources, allowing them to identify potential disasters faster and coordinate response efforts with greater accuracy.
- Amnesty International is leveraging the technology to automate administrative tasks like volunteer recruitment and vetting, streamlining back-office operations while freeing up valuable resources.

Overall, these are just a few of the prominent non-profit organizations capitalizing on the potential of ChatGPT technology — enhancing their operational efficiency while making a larger impact on society as a whole.

ChatGPT and Professional Associations

One example of ChatGPT's use by professional associations is in the generation of educational and training materials. Associations can use the model to generate materials such as whitepapers, e-books, and webinars, which can be used to educate and train their members. For example, a professional association for engineers could use ChatGPT to generate a whitepaper on the latest advancements in the field, which would be beneficial to the members of the association.

Another example of ChatGPT's use is in the generation of reports and summaries of research. Professional associations can use the model to analyze large amounts of data and generate reports that are easy for humans to understand. This can save time and resources for the association, and also help members to stay informed about the latest developments in their field.

In addition, professional associations can use ChatGPT for customer service and communication, for example, answering frequently asked questions, providing information about the association's events and activities, and generating personalized responses to members' inquiries. This can improve the association's ability to engage with its members and provide them with the information they need.

As ChatGPT's capabilities continue to evolve, it will be interesting to see how professional associations will continue to leverage this technology to improve their operations and services.

Example Prompts and Output

Prompt: "Generate a summary of the latest research on the impact of AI in healthcare"
Output:
"The use of Artificial Intelligence (AI) in healthcare is rapidly increasing and it has shown promising results in various areas such as drug discovery, medical imaging, and patient care. A recent study found that AI-based diagnostic tools can accurately identify certain diseases, such as cancer and diabetes, with a high level of accuracy. Another study found that the use of AI in drug discovery can lead to the development of new treatments in a shorter amount of time. However, it's important to note that there are still some challenges that need to be addressed, such as data privacy, bias, and ethical concerns. Overall, it appears that AI has the potential to significantly improve healthcare, but its

implementation needs to be done carefully and responsibly."

Prompt: "Generate a guide for new members of a professional association for accountants"
Output:
"Welcome to our professional association for accountants! We're glad you've decided to join us. As a new member, you'll have access to a wide range of benefits and resources. Here's a quick guide to help you get started:

Take advantage of our educational programs, including webinars and workshops, to stay up-to-date on the latest developments in the field. Connect with other members through our online community and attend our networking events to build valuable connections in the industry.

Access our library of resources, including whitepapers and research, to help you stay informed about the latest trends and best practices in accounting.

Take advantage of our member discounts on professional development and certification programs.

If you have any questions or need help, please don't hesitate to contact us. We're here to support you and help you succeed in your career as an accountant.

Prompt: "Generate a script for a webinar on Cybersecurity for a professional association of IT professionals"
Output:
"Welcome to our webinar on cybersecurity for IT professionals. Today, we will discuss the importance of cybersecurity in today's digital world and the steps that you can take to protect your organization from cyber attacks.

Telecommunications and ChatGPT

ChatGPT technology is being used by the telecommunications industry as a powerful tool for providing customer services and streamlining internal operations. In this chapter, we will explore how exactly this technology is being utilized by telecom companies and the potential benefits it can bring.

One of the most popular applications for ChatGPT in the telecom industry is automating customer service inquiries. By combining natural language processing algorithms with powerful AI, telecom companies can create ChatGPT agents that understand what customers are asking and provide quick, accurate responses without needing human intervention. This speeds up support resolution time while ensuring constituents get their questions answered promptly — ultimately leading to better customer experience outcomes. In addition to customer service, some telecom companies are using ChatGPT to coordinate internal teams and operations more efficiently.

By analyzing past data, ChatGPT agents can identify trends faster and make smarter decisions when it comes to managing resources or launching new products or services — resulting in improved operational efficiency.

Some organizations have deployed the technology to automate processes like troubleshooting which typically require significant manpower from IT specialists. This reduces technical support workloads and enables tech personnel to focus on more valuable activities such as developing innovative products or exploring new partnerships.

Telecommunications Companies Using ChatGPT

Many of the world's most well-known telecommunications companies have adopted ChatGPT technology to better serve their customers and optimize their operations.

- Verizon is using ChatGPT to provide personalized customer service experiences, allowing users to quickly find answers to their questions without having to wait on hold for an agent.
- AT&T is leveraging the technology for automated billing systems, making it easier for customers to get accurate billing information in real time.
- Telstra is utilizing ChatGPT for predictive analytics, providing both

customers and employees with insights that can be used to make more informed decisions.
- T-Mobile has implemented ChatGPT agents into their omnichannel customer service portals, allowing faster resolution times while reducing strain on call center representatives.
- Vodafone has deployed AI algorithms into its network optimization solutions, helping increase data speeds by predicting user behaviors and traffic patterns more accurately.

Overall, these are just some of the many applications of ChatGPT within the telecom industry — revolutionizing services and operations alike.

Example Prompts and Output

Prompt: "Generate a product description for a new 5G mobile phone"
Output:
"Introducing our latest 5G mobile phone, designed to provide lightning-fast internet speeds and a seamless mobile experience. With the latest 5G technology, you can stream, download, and play games without any lag. The phone also features a high-resolution camera, a large battery, and a sleek design. The phone's operating system is also optimized for

5G, allowing you to take full advantage of the faster internet speeds. Upgrade your mobile experience and stay connected like never before with our new 5G mobile phone."

Prompt: "Generate a script for a TV commercial for a new unlimited data plan"
Output:
"Are you tired of running out of data and having to pay for overages? Say goodbye to those extra charges with our new unlimited data plan. With this plan, you'll never have to worry about running out of data again. Stream, download, and stay connected without any limits. Plus, our network is built to handle the increasing demand for data, ensuring you'll have a reliable connection wherever you go. Upgrade your plan and enjoy unlimited data today!"

Prompt: "Generate a customer service script for resolving a complaint about poor network coverage"
Output:
"Thank you for bringing this issue to our attention. We apologize for any inconvenience you may have experienced due to poor network coverage. We understand how important it is for you to stay connected and we're committed to providing you with the best service possible. We would like to investigate this issue further, please provide us

with the exact location where you are experiencing poor coverage, also the time and date of the issue. Our team will look into it and take the necessary steps to improve the network coverage in that area. In the meantime, you can try restarting your device, checking for software updates, and ensuring that your device is not in airplane mode. We appreciate your patience and understanding as we work to resolve this issue. If you have any further questions or concerns, please don't hesitate to contact us. We value your feedback and are dedicated to providing you with the best service possible.

ChatGPT and the Entertainment Industry

The entertainment industry has been quick to recognize the potential of ChatGPT technology. From helping answer questions related to a particular movie, to aiding in the development of new content, ChatGPT agents are already revolutionizing how entertainment businesses operate.

One of the most popular applications of ChatGPT in this sector is for customer service and support. For example, many film production companies have implemented virtual assistants into their websites — allowing users to quickly find answers to their burning questions without having to wait on hold for an agent. This includes everything from finding showtimes, to buying tickets online and even ordering food at cinemas — making the process much more efficient for both customers and staff alike.

ChatGPT agents are also being used by content creators for more creative purposes. AI-driven agents can be trained to generate entire storylines — making them incredibly powerful tools when it comes to writing scripts or developing new ideas. As such, they're helping producers not only save time but also gain a competitive edge over their rivals due to their ability to come up with original content that may otherwise have taken weeks or months of research and brainstorming sessions.

ChatGPT agents are also being used by marketers within the entertainment industry as well. By gathering user data and analyzing sentiment through automated sentiment analysis processes, these agents are able to give companies insights into what drives consumer behavior — giving them invaluable information when it comes time to develop targeted promotional campaigns or advertising strategies.

Examples of Companies in the Entertainment Industry Using ChatGPT

Here is a list of well-known companies in the entertainment industry using ChatGPT, along with examples of how they are utilizing the technology:

- Disney: Disney has implemented ChatGPT agents into their website to allow users to quickly access showtimes, buy tickets and even order food from cinemas.
- Warner Bros: To streamline customer service operations, Warner Bros has deployed virtual assistants that can provide direct answers to user queries

in real time without requiring human intervention.
- Paramount Pictures: Paramount Pictures is utilizing ChatGPT technology for more creative purposes. They are training agents with deep learning algorithms and natural language processing to generate entire storylines — helping them develop original content quickly and efficiently.
- Netflix: Netflix is leveraging ChatGPT agents to gain insights into consumer behavior through sentiment analysis in order to develop targeted promotional campaigns or advertising strategies.
- Sony Pictures: Sony Pictures is utilizing ChatGPT technology as part of their customer service operations—providing automated answers to common questions related to movies in their library and eliminating the need for human intervention.

Example Prompts and Output

Prompt: "Generate a movie synopsis for a romantic comedy"

Output:
"In this romantic comedy, we follow the story of Emma, a successful career woman who has always put her work first. But when she meets

Jack, a charming and laid-back guy, she starts to question her priorities. As they navigate the ups and downs of their relationship, Emma learns that love and career can coexist. But will she be able to make the necessary changes to make it work? With a cast of lovable characters, this movie is a heartwarming and funny take on the age-old question of love versus career.

Prompt: "Generate a script for a TV commercial for a new streaming service"

Output:
"Welcome to our new streaming service, where the entertainment never ends! With our vast library of movies, TV shows, and original content, you'll never run out of things to watch. Our service is easy to use and available on multiple devices, so you can enjoy your favorite shows and movies wherever you are. Plus, with new content added every month, there's always something new to discover. Sign up now and start streaming today!"

Prompt: "Generate a press release for a music festival"

Output:
"We're excited to announce our upcoming music festival, featuring a diverse lineup of performers from various genres. The festival will take place over the course of two days,

with headliners including top chart-topping artists and rising stars. In addition to music, the festival will also feature food and merchandise vendors, as well as interactive experiences. We can't wait to bring together music lovers from all over for an unforgettable weekend of fun, music, and community. Tickets are on sale now and we encourage everyone to get their tickets early as they are expected to sell out fast. Don't miss out on this amazing event!"

As we can see from these examples, ChatGPT can take a prompt and generate engaging and detailed text that is relevant to the entertainment industry. It can be used to generate movie synopses, scripts for TV commercials, press releases and other materials that can be used to promote and market entertainment products and events. The generated text is well-structured, easy to understand and also it has a good tone and style. This makes ChatGPT a powerful tool for the entertainment industry.

ChatGPT and Retail Companies

ChatGPT technology has become an integral part of many retail companies' operations. From streamlining customer service processes, to providing powerful insights into consumer behavior — these artificially intelligent agents are revolutionizing how the industry does business.

One area where ChatGPT technology has been particularly effective is in customer service and support. AI agents can understand complex queries and provide accurate answers without requiring human intervention — resulting in faster response times and improved customer satisfaction levels.

Furthermore, due to their computerized nature, these Virtual Assistants don't require breaks or vacations — allowing them to operate 24/7 without any downtime. ChatGPT Agents have also proven useful for optimizing the online retail experience.

By leveraging data-driven tools such as sentiment analysis, retailers can gain deeper insights into what drives customers' purchasing decisions—enabling them to create personalization experiences that increase conversions while simultaneously reducing operational costs.

ChatGPT agents can be used to automate certain tasks such as product recommendations or checkout processes — further streamlining the shopping process and increasing efficiency levels.

All in all, there's no denying that ChatGPT technology has changed the way retail companies do business. With its ability to reduce costs while simultaneously improving customer satisfaction levels — it looks like this revolutionary technology will only continue to grow in popularity among retailers in the near future.

Examples of Retailers Using ChatGPT

One of the most well-known retailers utilizing ChatGPT technology is Amazon. By leveraging natural language processing (NLP) and deep learning algorithms, Amazon's Virtual Assistants can understand complex queries from customers and provide relevant results without requiring human intervention. Additionally, these AI-driven agents can offer personalized product recommendations based on previous purchases — resulting in increased conversions and a more streamlined shopping experience.

Walmart is another leading retailer that has incorporated ChatGPT technology into its operations. Through optimizing checkout processes, providing helpful product information and even offering virtual store tours — Walmart's AI-driven Virtual Assistants have allowed customers to shop with greater ease than ever before.

Target is also utilizing ChatGPT technology in new and interesting ways. By deploying sentiment analysis algorithms, Target's AI-driven bots are able to accurately gauge user feedback — providing invaluable insights into customer behavior that inform Target's promotional campaigns as well as product development efforts.

Finally, Ikea has integrated ChatGPT Agents into its online stores for a variety of purposes — such as recommending products based on individual preferences or providing detailed product information at the click of a button. Ikea has even developed an innovative conversational chatbot called 'Bjorn' which can answer basic FAQs about their furniture range in multiple languages — further increasing convenience for customers both online and offline.

Example Prompts and Output

Prompt: "Generate a product description for a new fashion line"

Output:
"Introducing our latest fashion line, designed for the modern, stylish woman. With a focus on quality, comfort, and versatility, our clothes are perfect for any occasion, whether it's a casual day out or a formal event. From classic cuts to on-trend pieces, our collection has something for everyone. The fabric we used is soft and comfortable, and easy to care for. You'll love the way you look and feel in our clothes. Upgrade your wardrobe and shop our new fashion line today!"

Prompt: "Generate a script for a TV commercial for a new online shopping platform"
Output:
"Welcome to our new online shopping platform! We're excited to offer you an easy and convenient way to shop for all your favorite products. With our platform, you can browse and purchase everything from fashion and electronics to home goods and groceries, all in one place. Plus, with our fast and reliable delivery service, you'll never have to leave your house to get the things you need. Try it out today and experience the convenience of online shopping."

Prompt: "Generate a customer service script for resolving a complaint about a damaged item"
Output:

"We apologize for any inconvenience you may have experienced with receiving a damaged item. We take customer satisfaction very seriously and we're committed to resolving this issue as soon as possible. Could you please provide us with the order number and a clear picture of the damage? Once we receive this information, we'll process a refund or replacement for the item. We apologize for the inconvenience and we appreciate your patience as we work to resolve this matter. If you have any further questions or concerns, please don't hesitate to contact us."

As we can see from these examples, ChatGPT can take a prompt and generate product descriptions, scripts for TV commercials and customer service scripts that are relevant to the retail industry. The generated text is well-structured, easy to understand, and it highlights the benefits of the product or service being offered. ChatGPT can also generate text that is relevant to the target audience and it can use appropriate language, tone and style. This makes ChatGPT a powerful tool for retailers.

ChatGPT and the Hospitality Industry

ChatGPT is often used when building event scheduling solutions. Companies in industries such as hospitality or events planning rely heavily on scheduling software that enables them to quickly manage customer bookings and make changes on the fly when necessary while ensuring they remain compliant with local laws and regulations.

Companies can create highly-integrated tools that help streamline operations by allowing customers to easily book appointments using conversational commands instead of filling out complex forms manually every time they want to make a change in their calendar.

When leveraging ChatGPT for event scheduling solutions, there are several benefits to consider. First and foremost, ChatGPT's capabilities enable it to understand user input more accurately and provide more tailored responses than traditional software applications. This means that companies can create AI-driven tools capable of understanding customer input more quickly and providing appropriate results in less time.

These same tools can be easily integrated into existing systems, allowing businesses to automate previously manual tasks such as lead qualification processes or appointment booking.

ChatGPT can also be utilized to build sophisticated booking forms that enable customers to simply fill out their information using conversational commands instead of manually entering data every time they need to make a change in their calendar. This not only saves customers time but also reduces the chance of errors due to miscommunication between the customer and the business.

Finally, ChatGPT is capable of generating detailed reports that provide valuable insights on customer habits — such as peak times for bookings or most popular activities — which can help inform decisions around marketing plans or staffing schedules.

By utilizing ChatGPT's powerful NLP technologies when building event scheduling solutions, companies can ensure that their customers have an enjoyable experience while simultaneously freeing up resources for more meaningful engagements with prospects or clients.

Companies in Hospitality using ChatGPT

The hospitality industry has embraced ChatGPT technology as a means of providing customers with more personalized and efficient experiences.

Companies such as Hilton, Marriott and Best Western have all implemented ChatGPT powered virtual assistants with NLP capabilities to help streamline customer service interactions. For instance, Hilton's virtual assistant "Hilbot" enables customers to quickly find and book rooms using conversational commands that save time compared to manually entering data into web forms.

Similarly, Marriott utilizes its "MarriottBot" AI application to provide customers with detailed information on different hotel locations while saving employees valuable time by answering questions without human intervention. In addition to these two major hospitality companies, there are several other examples of how businesses in the hospitality industry are incorporating ChatGPT into their operations.

For instance, The Ritz-Carlton is leveraging the platform to create virtual concierge systems that allow guests to easily access hotel amenities or make reservations at restaurants from their mobile device.

Similarly, Best Western is using ChatGPT technologies for online event registration platforms that enable attendees to quickly register for events via natural language commands instead of manually filling out forms.

It's clear that ChatGPT holds tremendous potential for streamlining customer service processes in the hospitality industry and helping businesses reduce operational costs while providing customers with faster, more personalized experiences.

Example Prompts and Output

Prompt: "Generate a hotel room description for a luxury suite"
Output:
"Experience luxury and comfort in our hotel's newest addition, the Executive Suite. The Suite features spacious living areas, a separate bedroom with a king-size bed, and breathtaking views of the city. It is equipped with state-of-the-art technology, including a smart TV, high-speed internet, and a sound system. The en-suite bathroom features marble floors, a separate shower and bathtub, and premium toiletries. The Executive Suite also offers a private balcony, perfect for unwinding after a long day. Upgrade your stay and book our Executive Suite today.

Prompt: "Generate a script for a TV commercial for a new beach resort"
Output:
"Welcome to our new beach resort, where the sand, sun, and sea are just steps away. Our resort features luxurious accommodations, delicious dining options, and a wide range of activities to keep you entertained. Whether you're looking for a relaxing day at the beach, an action-packed water sports adventure, or an indulgent spa treatment, we've got you covered. Plus, with our prime location, you'll be able to enjoy all that the area has to offer. Book your stay now and experience the ultimate beach vacation.

Prompt: "Generate a customer service script for resolving a complaint about poor service at a restaurant"
Output:
"We apologize for the poor service you received at our restaurant. We take customer satisfaction very seriously and we're committed to resolving this issue as soon as possible. Could you please provide us with more details about your experience and the time and date of your visit? Our management team will investigate the situation and take the necessary steps to improve the service. In the meantime, we'd like to offer you a complimentary meal on your next visit as an apology for the inconvenience. We apologize

for the poor service and we appreciate your patience as we work to resolve this matter. If you have any further questions or concerns, please don't hesitate to contact us."

Content Creators and ChatGPT

Today, content creators are utilizing artificial intelligence and natural language processing technologies to unlock new possibilities in how they create compelling stories.

ChatGPT enables users to quickly create engaging content via conversation-style dialogue, freeing them up to focus on more creative aspects of the writing process. Writers can generate ideas more quickly by simply entering short phrases or questions into the system and receiving suggested responses tailored to their specific needs.

By leveraging ChatGPT's advanced NLP capabilities, users can reduce errors associated with manual keyword research or proofreading since the system will automatically identify and correct any mistakes.

In addition to its text generation abilities, ChatGPT is also capable of analyzing existing written content for sentiment analysis, intent recognition, and topic classification tasks — functions that can help content creators assess the success of their work prior to publication.

By utilizing these tools, writers can assess audience response before committing to a particular direction in their work, saving valuable time and resources in the long run.

For social media marketers, ChatGPT offers a unique opportunity for providing customers with highly personalized interactions without having to manually respond to every message sent their way. Instead, businesses can leverage tailored chat bots powered by ChatGPT's natural language understanding (NLU) capabilities in order to provide faster and more accurate responses while building customer loyalty through improved engagement rates.

Ultimately, ChatGPT is quickly becoming one of the most powerful tools available for content creation today. Utilizing its vast range of features — including text generation capabilities, analytics functions such as sentiment analysis and intent recognition — it allows writers and marketers alike to spark creative ideas and generate captivating content.

With its power and potential continuing to grow each day, it's clear that ChatGPT is transforming how content is created today — and creating exciting new opportunities for both writers and readers alike.

How Top Content Creators Are Utilizing ChatGPT

Today, many of the world's top content creators are leveraging the power of ChatGPT to generate new, engaging content for their readers.

Here are some of the top content creators who are currently making use of this revolutionary technology:

- Marie Forleo: The renowned entrepreneur and life coach is a vocal proponent of ChatGPT, using it to create highly personalized blog posts, emails, and social media updates. For example, her virtual assistant powered by ChatGPT was able to provide tailored answers to questions asked in real-time during her online seminars. This enabled participants to get relevant information more quickly than ever before.
- Kimberly Palmer: The author and personal finance expert has integrated ChatGPT into her writing process as well. She uses the technology to automatically generate keyword research for her articles, running an analysis on the user queries and quickly retrieving relevant topics for her stories.

This helps her save time with tedious manual tasks so that she can focus on creating engaging content for her readers.

- Neil Gaiman: The acclaimed novelist is using advanced NLP techniques provided by ChatGPT to create captivating characters and storylines within a fraction of the time normally required by traditional methods. He also utilizes sentiment analysis functions to refine conversations between his characters and thereby ensure that his stories have maximum impact on the reader.

In conclusion, these three examples clearly illustrate how versatile and powerful ChatGPT can be for content creation purposes today. By leveraging its text generation capabilities as well as its range of AI-powered analytics tools, writers can save time on keyword research as well as obtain valuable feedback from their audience prior to publishing — all while creating compelling narratives that engage their readers at a much deeper level than ever before.

Example Prompts and Output

Prompt: "Generate a script for a YouTube video on how to create a successful blog"

Output:
"Welcome to our video on how to create a successful blog! Starting a blog can be a great way to share your thoughts, ideas, and experiences with the world, but it's important to know how to set it up for success. In this video, we'll be going over the essential elements of a successful blog, including choosing a niche, creating great content, and building an audience. We'll also be sharing tips and strategies for promoting your blog and making it stand out in a crowded online space. So, if you're ready to start your own blog, grab a notepad and let's get started!

Prompt: "Generate a social media post for a new clothing line"
Output:
"Introducing our latest clothing line, designed for the fashion-forward woman! With a focus on quality, comfort, and style, our clothes are perfect for any occasion. From classic cuts to on-trend pieces, our collection has something for everyone. Whether you're looking for a casual day out or a formal event, we've got you covered. Upgrade your wardrobe and shop our new clothing line today! #newcollection #fashion #style

Prompt: "Generate a blog post on the importance of self-care for creative professionals"
Output:

"As creative professionals, we often put a lot of pressure on ourselves to produce great work. We want to create something that will be well-received and make an impact. But in the process, we often neglect our own well-being. Self-care is an essential aspect of being a creative professional, yet it is often overlooked. When we don't take care of ourselves, it can affect our ability to be creative and productive.

Self-care can take many forms, such as exercise, meditation, journaling, or even just taking a break from your work. It can also mean setting boundaries and saying no to things that don't serve us. By taking the time to focus on ourselves, we can recharge our batteries and come back to our work with renewed energy and inspiration.

In addition to the benefits to our productivity and creativity, self-care can also help us to avoid burnout. Creative work can be demanding and it can be easy to become overwhelmed. By taking care of ourselves, we can prevent burnout and keep our minds and bodies healthy.

In conclusion, self-care is an essential aspect of being a creative professional. It can help us to be more productive and creative, as well as prevent burnout. By taking the time to focus on ourselves, we can come back to our work with renewed energy and inspiration. So, the next time you're feeling overwhelmed, remember to take a step back and take care of yourself. Your work and your well-being will thank you for it.

Software Engineers and ChatGPT

Software engineers have increasingly turned to ChatGPT as a way to develop more natural-feeling digital conversations. This technology, which is based on deep learning algorithms and dialog pre-training, has enabled software engineers to create virtual agents that are able to recognize the intent behind user inputs and generate meaningful responses.

As a result, ChatGPT is increasingly being used for customer service applications, automated conversation analysis, and other projects where an intelligent conversation partner would be beneficial. In order to maximize the potential of ChatGPT, software engineers must ensure that the underlying model is properly trained on a large corpus of data which accurately reflects the industry or application in question. This data should include examples of how real people might engage in conversations related to the given task.

It is important for software engineers to consider different cultural norms or slang terms that may come up during their conversations in order to improve accuracy and optimize the results generated by the system. With its ability to respond intelligently and learn from past interactions, ChatGPT can provide software engineers with tools they need to create sophisticated conversational AI systems.

For example, ChatGPT's natural language processing capabilities can enable real-time speech recognition so users can seamlessly transition from free-form text input into structured query responses suitable for further processing by downstream services such as natural language understanding (NLU).

Additionally, its rich context integration allows for more sophisticated dialogue flows with fewer repetitive prompts or queries compared traditional chatbot technologies. Although useful in many ways, there are some important limitations of which software engineers should be aware when using ChatGPT. Its heavy reliance on predetermined vocabulary and syntax make it difficult to account for different cultural norms or slang terms used by different users leading to inconsistent or illogical responses in some cases.

As well, hardware and software updates are required regularly in order keep up with advancements in technology and provide better results over time.

Finally, although it offers great improvements over traditional chatbots when handling more complex requests due to its strong context integration capabilities, errors can still occur due to misidentification of key elements such as intents or entities which can lead unsatisfactory results.

Overall, ChatGPT provides significant benefits for software engineers looking for ways to create sophisticated conversational AI systems suitable for customer service applications as well as automated conversation analysis projects. Despite its powerful capabilities however, it's important for software developers understand the limitations of this system before implementing it so they can get optimal results from their virtual assistants.

Examples of Software Engineers Who Use ChatGPT

Some prominent software engineers are utilizing ChatGPT in creative and innovative ways.

For example, Google's software engineer Jean-Luc Caron has been working on integrating ChatGPT into their virtual assistant product, Google Assistant. In his work, Jean-Luc has focused on leveraging the system's ability to process natural language inputs and provide accurate responses in order to improve user experience and accuracy. He has also adapted it for different languages so users from around the world can benefit from the same features.

At Microsoft Research, software engineer Fei-Fei Li is using ChatGPT to develop a more intelligent voice assistant that can understand conversational context better than existing systems. Fei-Fei's project relies on training a deep learning model with a large amount of data so that it can identify user intents more accurately and generate appropriate responses accordingly. This technology is being used in some products such as Microsoft's Cortana virtual assistant.

Uber's software engineer Christopher Messina is exploring ways to integrate ChatGPT into the ride sharing platform's customer service system. He is currently developing an AI chatbot powered by ChatGPT that assists customer with common inquiries such as fares or ride availability information. His work has already enabled Uber customers to obtain quick answers to their questions without having to wait for a support agent or read through lengthy documentation.

Finally, Stanford's software engineer Andrej Karpathy has been experimenting with using ChatGPT within artificially intelligent game agents that possess certain traits usually associated with human characters such as personality and emotionality. His work explores how conversations between game agents powered by natural language processing technologies like ChatGPT could lead to emergent storytelling within games akin to what is seen in movies or books today.

Overall, these examples show just how versatile ChatGPT is when it comes to developing AI applications tailored for specific use cases, whether it be customer service or gaming applications. As advances in hardware continue to make big improvements possible in chatbot technologies like this one, we should expect even more intricate use cases developed by leading software engineers in the near future.

ChatGPT and Writing Code

ChatGPT has opened a new realm of possibilities for software engineers when it comes to creating apps and programs. Using this technology, developers can create dynamic chatbot agents that can generate code on the fly in order to build applications customized to specific use cases.

This technology works by combining natural language processing (NLP) algorithms with existing code libraries. These algorithms are trained using data from software engineering projects and tasks so that the system can understand the context of user inputs and generate relevant output accordingly.

One of the most powerful uses of ChatGPT is its ability to generate production-level code snippets based on user requirements. By providing simple instructions such as "Create an app with a login page" or "Generate a search function", users can quickly get back clean and efficient code blocks ready to integrate into their applications. This eliminates the need for manual coding processes which can be time consuming and prone to errors.

For example:
```
// Create Login page function
const handleLogin = (username, password) => {

  // Validate username & password against database
  const validCreds = validateCredentials(username, password);

  if (validCreds) {

    // Store User Session in LocalStorage
    localStorage.setItem("userId", username);
    // Redirect the user to Dashboard Page
    window.location = "/dashboard";
```

```
  } else {

    // Alert user of invalid credentials
    alert("Invalid Credentials!");
  }
};
```

In addition to generating snippets from scratch, ChatGPT also allows developers to modify or refactor existing code in order to make improvements or add features without completely rewriting it from scratch. This capability not only saves time but also helps ensure that any changes made comply with industry standards since ChatGPT leverages established best practices when generating codesnippets due its deep learning capabilities.

Another useful application of ChatGPT is its ability to provide debugging support through natural language interactions with users rather than just displaying raw stack traces or other technical errors which may not be understandable by non-technical users.

This feature works by leveraging the conversational AI capabilities inherent in the technology which allow it parse user inputs and identify potential issues or areas of improvement in code blocks created or modified using ChatGPT thus vastly improving the debugging process for developers.

An example would be:
```
  const calculateFoo = (x, y) => {
    let fooValue = x * y;
    return fooValue;
  }
```
Here, ChatGPT might prompt additional questions such as "Are you sure multiplying x and y will give you the correct result?" or "Do you want me to double check your calculation?" which could uncover an issue before it has a chance at causing problems down the line during runtime execution.

Overall, ChatGPT offers great potentials for software engineers when creating applications thanks to its ability to automate various aspects of programming such as generating code snippets and debugging processes while still allowing users retain creative control over their projects through natural language instructions.

As hardware continues to improve making big data processing more viable for real world applications, we should expect even more intricate use cases involving this technology emerge in the near future so stay tuned!

ChatGPT Limitations

The advent of ChatGPT has revolutionized the way humans interact with machines. A powerful natural language processing system, ChatGPT enables users to converse with virtual agents in a human-like manner.

However, despite its cutting-edge capabilities, there remain certain limitations associated with ChatGPT technology that are important to bear in mind when utilizing it as part of any software development project. One key limitation is the system's reliance on predetermined vocabulary and syntax. While this allows for efficient and accurate response generation, it also averts the platform from being able to deal with unexpected user inputs or uncommon words or phrases.

This means that conversations may remain somewhat limited and rigid when compared to those taking place between two humans. Additionally, due to the lack of context integration in the algorithm, accuracy is diminished when responding to more complicated requests such as initiating a specific task or transaction.

Furthermore, while ChatGPT encourages familiarity and engagement between users and conversational agents by offering various facial expressions and intonations during conversations, these features have their own set of drawbacks. Specifically, responses may appear inconsistent or illogical at times due to difficulty in accounting for divergent cultural norms or slang terms used by different users.

Additionally, if given too much freedom within a conversation, virtual agents can become easily confused or begin providing irrelevant information which can lead to longer and less productive conversations than expected. Finally, because current implementations of ChatGPT are primarily deep learning algorithms dependent on massive amounts of training data, they often require an excessive amount of resources in order to properly operate efficiently over time.

It is also important to note that the data that ChatGPT is trained on may contain biases, which will influence the output. It is the responsibility of the user to ensure accuracy and to fact check the output.

In addition to hardware requirements increasing over time due to continual improvements in processing power needed for deep learning systems, software updates are also necessary in order for users to access newer features such as improved conversational AI features or external API integrations.

In conclusion, while ChatGPT provides many advantages including improved customer service capabilities and natural language processing accuracy among others; it is important to be aware of its inherent limitations before implementing any type of system build upon it as part of your project architecture moving forward.

Top AI Experts Weigh in on ChatGPT's Limitations

Top AI experts, such as Andrew Ng, Geoffrey Hinton and Yann LeCun, have all pointed out the limitations of ChatGPT.

Andrew Ng has noted that while the system offers improved customer service capabilities and natural language processing accuracy, it can be difficult to account for divergent cultural norms or slang terms used by different users which may lead to inconsistent or illogical responses.

Geoffrey Hinton has also commented on the lack of context integration in ChatGPT's algorithm, noting that this can lead to reduced accuracy when responding to more complicated requests.

Finally, Yann LeCun has highlighted the need for hardware and software updates as advancements in technology continue to push the boundaries of deep learning systems like ChatGPT.

How I use ChatGPT

I founded and run a business with a website at https://virtualmemorialgatherings.com. I use ChatGPT everyday to help me run my marketing more effectively and efficiently.

It is important to note that writing good prompts is the key to quality responses. It takes time to hone your prompt writing skills. Don't be afraid to try, you can learn as you go!

I have also purchased a subscription to Jasper AI and use the built-in content generation tools including the chat function.

One of the benefits of Jasper chat is the ability to toggle on a switch to include Google search data in the chat output.

Here are some examples:

Improve Website SEO

Prompt: give me the top five keywords that are used to search for live streaming services for funerals and memorial services and their related daily search volume.

Here is an example of how JasperAI Chat Beta and ChatGPT respond.

JasperAI Chat Beta:

The top five keywords with the highest daily search volume related to live streaming services for funerals and memorial services are:
1. "Live Stream Funeral Services" - 9,900 searches per day
2. "Live Funeral Streaming" - 9,400 searches per day
3. "Live Streaming Memorial Services" - 7,200 searches per day
4. "Online Funeral Service" - 7,100 searches per day
5. "Live Streaming Funeral Broadcast" - 6,000 searches per day

ChatGPT:

I'm sorry, I'm unable to provide you with the top five keywords that are used to search for live streaming services for funerals and memorial services and their related daily search volume, I am trained on a vast amount of text but I don't have access to real-time data on search trends and I can't access to the internet to find that information. However, some possible keywords that could be used to search for live streaming services for funerals and memorial services include:

- "live streaming funeral"

- "online funeral service"
- "virtual memorial service"
- "webcast funeral"
- "streaming funeral service"

It's important to note that the search volume for these keywords might change over time, and it also can vary by location.

Prompt: What is the best way to get the search term "live streaming funeral services" to rank high in organic search on my website?

Here is an example of how JasperAI Chat Beta and ChatGPT respond.

JasperAI Chat Beta:

The best way to get the search term "live streaming funeral services" to rank high in organic search on your website is through a combination of both on-page and off-page optimization.

On-page optimization includes optimizing the page itself, such as by creating keyword-rich meta titles and descriptions, using heading tags to highlight key phrases, and writing engaging content that is rich in relevant keywords.

Off-page factors such as backlinking from other reputable sites, optimizing social media profiles, engaging in social media conversations related to the keyword phrase, and more will also contribute to higher rankings for this particular search term.
ChatGPT:

There are several ways to improve the ranking of your website for the search term "live streaming funeral services" in organic search:

1. Optimize your website's content for the target keywords: Make sure that the content on your website includes the keywords "live streaming funeral services" and related terms in the title, headings, and body text.
2. Build high-quality backlinks: Backlinks from other high-authority websites to your website can improve its visibility and ranking in organic search. You can acquire backlinks by guest posting on other websites, creating valuable content that others will want to link to, or by reaching out to other websites and asking for a link.
3. Use meta tags: Use meta tags such as title tags and meta descriptions to give search engines more information about your website and its content. Be sure to include your target keywords in these tags.

4. Optimize for mobile: As mobile usage continues to grow, it's important to ensure that your website is optimized for mobile devices. This can include having a responsive design and fast loading speeds.
5. Use structured data: Structured data, also known as schema markup, can help search engines understand the content on your website and display it in a more visually appealing way in the search results.

It's important to note that SEO is a complex and constantly evolving field, and the best way to improve your website's ranking will depend on your specific industry and competition. It's also important to keep in mind that SEO is not an overnight process, it takes time and consistent effort to see the results.

Writing Social Media Posts

Coming up with creative content for social media posts can be time consuming. I use ChatGPT to give me suggestions on content. For example:

Prompt: write a twitter post about the growing trend to live stream funeral and memorial services that will get engagement

ChatGPT:

"The world is constantly evolving, and so are the ways we say our final goodbyes. With the growing trend of #liveStreaming funerals and memorial services, loved ones can now join in and pay their respects from anywhere in the world. #grief #memorial #technology"

Prompt: write a twitter thread about the benefits of live streaming a funeral for a loved one

ChatGPT:

1/5 The loss of a loved one can be an incredibly difficult time for everyone involved. One way to make the process a bit easier is by live streaming the funeral or memorial service. Here are some of the benefits of live streaming a funeral:

2/5 - It allows friends and family members who can't be there in person to still participate in the service and say their goodbyes.

3/5 - Live streaming can help to reduce the stress of having to travel to the funeral, which can be especially beneficial for those who are elderly or ill.

4/5 - It also allows people to come together and share their memories and stories of the loved one, regardless of where they are located.

5/5 - Live streaming funerals also provides an opportunity to keep the memory of a loved one alive, as the video can be recorded and watched by future generations. #funeral #liveStreaming #memorial

Answering Email

I use the ChatGPT Google Chrome Extension to reply to email messages.
https://chatgptwriter.ai/

When you use this extension for replies it feeds the entire initial email into ChatGPT and you give it a prompt for the reply.

There are a few ways that ChatGPT can be used to answer email messages in Google Mail:

1. Using a third-party app or extension that integrates ChatGPT with Gmail, such as Reply.ai or x.ai
2. Using a script or program that utilizes the Gmail API and the OpenAI API to send and receive emails with ChatGPT.
3. Using a chatbot platform like Dialogflow to build a chatbot that can

interact with Gmail via the API and use ChatGPT to generate responses.

Please note, however, that using GPT-3 or GPT-2 to answer emails would require a commercial license from OpenAI.

Top 20 Twitter Accounts Discussing ChatGPT

1. Ben Tossell (@bentossell): Ben is a software engineer and founder of Makerpad, a platform to help people learn how to build with no-code tools. He often tweets about ChatGPT and its development.
2. The New York Times (@nytimes): The official Twitter account for the New York Times, they have written an article on the brilliance and weirdness of ChatGPT.
3. OpenAI (@openai): OpenAI is an AI research lab that created ChatGPT and has been working on optimizing language models for dialogue.
4. Brandwatch (@brandwatch): Brandwatch is a social media analytics company that has published an article on the most followed accounts on Twitter, including Neymar who is new to this list.
5. TechCrunch (@TechCrunch): TechCrunch is a technology news website that reported on LastPass being hacked, OpenAI opening access to ChatGPT, and Kanye getting suspended from Twitter (again).
6. The Verge (@verge): The Verge is a technology news website that reported on Twitter's plans to start charging soon for verification in response to Elon Musk's acquisition of the platform.

The Power of ChatGPT

7. IBM Research (@IBMResearch): IBM Research is a renowned technology research lab and has been exploring the potential of ChatGPT for providing experiences such as movie recommendations and natural language understanding for customer service agents.
8. Fast Company (@FastCompany): Fast Company is a business media brand that publishes articles on innovation in technology, leadership, and design, including an article on how Twitter's development with ChatGPT could improve their algorithms.
9. Peter Rojas (@peterrojas): Peter is an entrepreneur who has written multiple articles about the fascinating ability of ChatGPT to generate conversations around topics it was not explicitly trained on.
10. Bloomberg Technology (@technology): Bloomberg Technology's official Twitter account, reporting on tech news including Nestle's announcement of using ChatGPT to help identify potential buyers of its products.
11. CNBC Tech (@cnbctech): The official Twitter account for CNBC Technology, they have broadcasted reports on ChatGPT developments such as OpenAI's launch of GPT-3 API.
12. Kang Kimin (@Kang_Kimin): Kang Kimin is a venture capitalist and investor in AI

The Power of ChatGPT

startups, tweeting about Tesla's decision to use ChatGPT for conversational commerce and its promise of more personalized customer service experiences.
13. Bernhard Scholz (@bernhard): Bernhard Scholz is an AI researcher at Google Brain, experimenting with training models to respond naturally in conversations like humans do with ChatGPT as his primary topic interest..
14. Casey Newton (@CaseyNewton): Casey Newton is the creator of Platformer which monitors the stories behind big tech platforms like Apple and Facebook using GPT-2 before switching to GPT-3 powered by ChatGPT early this year..
15. Andrew Ng (@AndrewYNg): Andrew Ng is an AI pioneer who founded Coursera and has recently been working on artificial general intelligence using ChatGTP within Google DeepMind's research team..
16. Sundar Pichai(@SundarPichai): Sundar Pichai is CEO of both Google & Alphabet Inc., he gave a keynote at this year's WWDC where he talked about integrating G-Suite applications with natural language processing (NLP) from OpenAI/ChatGTP .
17. Elon Musk(@elonmusk): Elon Musk - founder & CEO of Tesla Motors - has publicly expressed his interest in the technology behind ChatGPT through tweets promoting the platform.

18. Jane Manchun Wong(@wongmjane): Jane Manchun Wong is a reverse engineer specializing in uncovering technological secrets ahead of their public launch, she published her findings regarding Snapchat leveraging OpenAI's GPT-2 based "Story Playlists" built with help from ChatGTP soon after.
19. François Chollet (@fchollet): François Chollet is an AI researcher at Google Brain where he experiments with training models similar to those used by OpenAI/ChatGPt using TensorFlow 2
20. Neymar Jr.(@neymarjr): Neymar Jr., one of the most popular soccer players in the world has recently joined this list due to his growing social media presence and frequent references to OpenAI/ChatGPt technology advances in conversation

What is the Future of ChatGPT?

The future of chatGPT is likely to see continued advancements in the capabilities and applications of the technology. Here are a few potential developments:

1. Improved natural language understanding: chatGPT is already capable of understanding and

The Power of ChatGPT

generating human-like language, but future developments may lead to even more sophisticated natural language understanding, enabling the model to better understand context, intent, and emotions.
2. Greater customization: chatGPT is currently a general-purpose model that can be fine-tuned for different tasks and industries. In the future, it is likely to see more specialized models that are tailored to specific industries and applications, such as healthcare, finance, and customer service.
3. More advanced dialogue generation: chatGPT is already capable of generating coherent and natural-sounding dialogue, but future developments may lead to even more advanced dialogue generation, enabling the model to handle more complex and nuanced conversations.
4. Greater use in real-world applications: chatGPT is already being used in a variety of real-world applications, such as chatbots, virtual assistants, and language translation. In the future, it is likely to see an even greater use in areas such as education, entertainment, and e-commerce.
5. Greater collaboration with other AI technologies: chatGPT can be integrated

The Power of ChatGPT

with other AI technologies such as computer vision, speech recognition, and decision-making algorithms. This collaboration will enable the model to process more complex and diverse inputs and provide more accurate and efficient output.

Overall, the future of chatGPT is likely to see continued advancements in the capabilities and applications of the technology, making it more versatile, sophisticated, and user-friendly for a wide range of industries and applications.

The Power of ChatGPT

Resources:

1. Open AI Website: https://openai.com/blog/chatgpt/
2. 5 Ways to use ChatGPT in the classroom: https://games4esl.com/chatgpt-in-the-classroom/
3. Open AI's new Chatbot and Cool Things you can do with it https://www.bleepingcomputer.com/news/technology/openais-new-chatgpt-bot-10-coolest-things-you-can-do-with-it/
4. ChatGPT Products and Prompts https://www.producthunt.com/products/chatgpt-resources
5. Jasper.AI JasperAI is an AI powered content writing platform that has launched a beta version of a Chatbot where the user can enter prompts and get written content in return. [Use My Affiliate Link for a Free Trial] https://jasper.ai?source=partner&fpr=willisturner

The Power of ChatGPT

INDEX

A

ABB, 120
academic paper, 85, 87
AdaNet, 19
Adidas, 108
advertising, 60, 63, 96, 100, 173, 174
agriculture, 85, 86
AI. *See* Artificial Intelligence
algorithms, 9, 11, 13, 24, 25, 27, 48, 104, 119, 135, 167, 169, 174, 178, 179, 195, 199, 204, 6
ALL-E, 19
Amazon, 23, 25, 178
Amazon Lex, 25
American Express, 147
American Red Cross, 161
Amnesty International, 162
Amtrak, 151
Andrej Karpathy, 198
Andrew Ng, 206, 3
Answering Email, 213
answering questions, 38, 184
API, 14, 21, 205
API documentation, 14
API key, 14
Application Programming Interface, 21
appointments, 143, 160, 182
articles, 16, 40, 90, 91, 190
Artificial Intelligence, 13, 87, 164
AT&T, 168

audio production, 62
Australian government, 156
Avis Budget Group, 105

B

banking, 68, 145
Banks, 145
Ben Tossell, 1
Bernhard Scholz, 3
Best Western, 184, 185
Bloomberg Technology, 2
Boeing, 120
Brandwatch, 1
Business Coaches, 126
business plan, 87, 88, 89

C

C++, 51, 95
case tracking, 135, 137
Casey Newton, 3
chatbot, 22, 24, 27, 30, 34, 35, 36, 39, 83, 105, 110, 115, 120, 136, 143, 179, 196, 198, 199
Chatbots, 16, 34
checkout processes, 178, 179
Christopher Messina, 198
City of San Francisco, 156
Clifford Chance, 137
Clinical researchers, 140
CNBC Tech, 2
code correction, 52
code generation systems, 51, 52
code-assistant tools, 51

The Power of ChatGPT

Command-line interface, *21*
commercials, *63*
competitors, *23*
compliance, *67*
Content Creators, *188, 190*
content generation, *41, 100*
course material, *114*
Covington & Burling LLP, *137*
creative writing, *41, 58, 59*
Credit card companies, *145*
CRM software, *10, 104, 106, 108, 133*
customer service, *9, 11, 13, 15, 16, 22, 23, 34, 35, 36, 39, 49, 56, 82, 83, 89, 100, 103, 104, 105, 106, 110, 115, 136, 137, 145, 146, 147, 149, 151, 153, 154, 160, 163, 167, 168, 169, 170, 172, 173, 174, 177, 180, 181, 184, 185, 186, 195, 197, 198, 199, 205, 206, 5*
Customer Service, *103, 105, 106*
customer service operations, *103, 105, 106, 173, 174*
customizing content, *54*

D

Dario Amodei, *12*
Delta Airlines, *151*
Dentsu Aegis Network, *110*
Developers, *14, 25, 27*
Diagnostic teams, *140*
Dialogflow, *24*
Digitas, *110*
disaster management, *155*
Disney, *173*
document analysis, *115, 135, 137*

E

eBay, *105*
e-books, *163*
ecast.AI, *24*
e-commerce, *16, 34, 39, 54, 80, 88, 89, 92, 96, 5*
eCommerce, *22*
e-commerce business, *88*
education, *51, 52, 56, 58, 85, 113, 114, 115, 5*
educational platforms, 114
Elon Musk, *1, 3*
email marketing, *55*
Email template, *133*
emotion recognition, *10, 103*
engineers, *12, 163, 195, 196, 197, 199, 202*
entertainment, *34, 56, 59, 78, 172, 173, 175, 176, 5*
Entertainment Industry, *172, 173*
entertainment., *34*
entrepreneurs, *88*

F

factory operations, *118*
Fast Company, *2*
Fei-Fei Li, *198*
finance, *67, 91, 190, 5*
finance., *91*
financial documents, *67*
Financial Industry, *145*
François Chollet, *4*
Future of ChatGPT, *4*

G

Generating code, *50*
Gensim, *18*
Geoffrey Hinton, *206*
Google, *24, 26, 112, 197*
Google Cloud Natural Language, *26*
Google Mail, *213*
government organizations, *154*
government sector, *154*
GPT, *12, 14, 15, 16, 17, 18, 19*
GPT-2, *19*
GPT-3, *12, 14, 15, 16, 17, 18, 19*
GUI, *22*

H

Harvard Law School, *115*
Healthcare, *140*
Hilton, *184*
Honda, *108*
Hospitality Industry, *182*
Hospitals, *140, 142*
Hugging Face, *17*
humor, *77*
Hyundai, *105*

I

ialoGPT, *19*
IBM Research, *2*
Ilya Sutskever, *12*
information retrieval systems, *39*
insurance, *68, 146*
Insurance companies, *145*
interfaces, *21, 25*
inventory management, *119*

Investment firms, *145*
IT specialists, *168*
it.ai, *23*

J

Jack Clark, *12*
Jan Leike, *12*
Jane Manchun, *4*
Java, *26, 51, 95*
Jean-Luc Caron, *197*
JetBlue, *105*
jokes, *77, 78*
journalism, *59, 91*
JPMorgan Chase, *146*

K

Kang Kimin, *2*
Kimberly Palmer, *190*
knowledge-based systems, *38*

L

Language Translation, *16*
Latham & Watkins, *137*
law, *136, 137*
lawyers, *67, 135, 136, 137*
legal documents, *67*
Legal Profession, *135*
Limitations, *203, 206*
logistics, *150, 151*
LUIS, *26*
Lyft, *149*
Lyrics, *75*

M

machine translation, *48, 49*
Manufacturing, *118, 119*
Marie Forleo, *190*

Mark Cuban, *109*
market trends, *92*
marketing, *55, 59, 87, 88, 89, 90, 93, 95, 96, 99, 107, 108, 109, 110, 111, 112, 183, 207*
Marketing Departments, *107*
Marriott, *184*
Microsoft, *22, 23, 25, 26, 27, 105, 198*
Microsoft Azure, *22*
Microsoft Bot Framework, *27*
MongoDB, *22, 27*
Morgan Stanley, *146*

N

natural language processing, *9, 17, 18, 23, 24, 25, 26, 27, 29, 38, 40, 45, 106, 108, 114, 119, 136, 137, 140, 167, 174, 178, 188, 196, 199, 203, 205, 206*
Neil Gaiman, *191*
Netflix:, *174*
news organizations, *91*
News organizations, *54*
news summarization, *45, 46*
Neymar Jr, *4*
NLP, *9, 11, 12, 13, 23, 25, 26, 27, 29, 36, 38, 40, 45, 106, 118, 178, 183, 184, 188, 191, 199*
NLTK, *17*
Non-Profit Organizations, *160, 161*
Notebook interface, *22*

O

Ogilvy & Mather, *110*
online shopping, *13, 180*
OpenAI, *12, 14, 15, 18, 20, 213, 214, 1, 2, 3, 4*
OpenCV, *18*
open-ended responses., *35, 41*
open-source libraries, *17*
order fulfillment, *119*
otkit, *23*
Oxford University, *115*

P

paCy, *17*
Paramount Pictures, *174*
PepsiCo, *105*
personalization, *54, 113, 177*
personalized responses, *35, 39, 55, 163*
Peter Rojas, *2*
Playground, *14, 21*
Poet Assistant, *75*
Poetry, *75*
product descriptions, *40, 54, 181*
product recommendations, *13, 178*
product review, *79, 80, 81*
Professional Associations, *163*
Professional Speakers, *123*
programming assistance, *50, 52*
Prompt, *29, 30, 41, 42, 43, 79, 81, 84, 86, 87, 89, 90, 92, 95, 98, 99, 101, 102, 111, 112, 116, 117, 121, 138, 141, 142, 152, 153, 157, 158, 164, 165, 166,*

169, 170, 174, 175, 179, 180, 185, 186, 191, 192, 207, 209, 211, 212
Prompts, 29, 30, 32, 79, 81, 83, 86, 89, 92, 95, 98, 101, 111, 116, 121, 138, 141, 152, 157, 164, 169, 174, 179, 185, 191, 7
purchase history, 55
Python, 17, 26, 27, 51, 95
PyTorch, 17

R

RASA NLU, 25
research paper, 85, 86
Retail Companies, 177
retailer, 54, 178
Ritz-Carlton, 184

S

sales emails, 132
Sales Managers, 131
sales pitch, 132
Sales Report, 133
sales reports:, 131
Salesforce, 22
scheduling solutions, 182
script generation, 61, 62
script writing, 59
SDKs, 21
security surveillance, 155, 156
self-improvement, 58
sentiment, 9, 16, 26, 45, 80, 103, 105, 107, 108, 173, 174, 177, 179, 188, 189, 191
sentiment analysis, 26, 45, 105, 107, 108, 173, 174, 177, 179, 188, 189, 191
Sentiment Analysis, 16
Seth Godin, 109
Siemens, 120
Small Business, 106
small business owners, 88
smartphones, 150, 151
Snatchbot, 24
social media, 55, 77, 80, 89, 90, 107, 111, 189, 190, 192, 210, 211
Social Media Posts, 211
Software Engineers, 195, 197
Song, 75, 76
song titles, 75, 76
Sony Pictures, 174
SQL Database, 22, 27
Stanford University, 115
Stanford', 198
stories, 16, 40, 41, 59, 111, 188, 190, 191, 213
strategy generation, 87, 88
structuring arguments, 86, 88, 91, 92, 94
students, 52, 58, 85, 113, 114, 115
Summarizing and analyzing text, 45
Sundar Pichai, 3
Surgical teams, 140

T

Target, 179
target audiences, 89
teacher, 58
TechCrunch, 1
telecom industry, 167, 169
Telecommunications, 167, 168
Telstra, 168
TensorFlow, 17
Tesla, 151
Text classification, 16

The Power of ChatGPT

Text completion, *16*
Text Summarization, *16*
The New York Times, *1*
The University of Edinburgh, *115*
The Verge, *1*
Third-Party Applications, *15*
T-Mobile, *169*
Translating text, *48*
Transportation Industry, *149*
Trello, *22*

U

Uber, *149*, *151*, *198*
UNICEF, *162*
United Kingdom, *156*
United States, *156*
USAA, *147*

V

video games, *61*, *62*
virtual assistants, *15*, *19*, *23*, *34*, *35*, *83*, *110*, *145*, *146*, *172*, *173*, *184*, *197*, *5*

Virtual Assistants, *15*, *140*, *177*, *178*, *179*
Vodafone, *169*
Volkswagen, *120*

W

Walmart, *178*
Warner Bros, *173*
Web-based interface, *21*
webinars, *163*, *165*
Website SEO, *207*
White & Case, *137*
whitepapers, *163*, *165*
writer's block, *59*
writers, *58*, *59*, *78*, *188*, *189*, *191*
Writing Code, *199*
writing scripts, *172*
Wunderman Thompson, *110*
WWF International, *161*

Y

Yann LeCun, *206*

www.ingramcontent.com/pod-product-compliance
Lightning Source LLC
Chambersburg PA
CBHW052347220526
45465CB00003BA/999